D1031173

**UPDATED EDITION**

# BATHROOM IDEAS YOU CAN USE

## The Latest Design Styles, Fixtures, Surfaces and Remodeling Tips

### CHRIS PETERSON

COOL
SPRINGS
PRESS

Brimming with creative inspiration, how-to projects, and useful information to enrich your everyday life, Quarto Knows is a favorite destination for those pursuing their interests and passions. Visit our site and dig deeper with our books into your area of interest: Quarto Creates, Quarto Cooks, Quarto Homes, Quarto Lives, Quarto Drives, Quarto Explores, Quarto Gifts, or Quarto Kids.

© 2018 Quarto Publishing Group USA Inc. Text © 2013, 2018

First published in 2013 by Cool Springs Press, an imprint of The Quarto Group, 401 Second Avenue North, Suite 310, Minneapolis, MN 55401 USA. This edition published in 2018. T (612) 344-8100 F (612) 344-8692 www.QuartoKnows.com

All rights reserved. No part of this book may be reproduced in any form without written permission of the copyright owners. All images in this book have been reproduced with the knowledge and prior consent of the artists concerned, and no responsibility is accepted by producer, publisher, or printer for any infringement of copyright or otherwise, arising from the contents of this publication. Every effort has been made to ensure that credits accurately comply with information supplied. We apologize for any inaccuracies that may have occurred and will resolve inaccurate or missing information in a subsequent reprinting of the book.

Cool Springs Press titles are also available at discount for retail, wholesale, promotional, and bulk purchase. For details, contact the Special Sales Manager by email at specialsales@quarto.com or by mail at The Quarto Group, Attn: Special Sales Manager, 401 Second Avenue North, Suite 310, Minneapolis, MN 55401 USA.

10 9 8 7 6 5 4 3 2

ISBN: 978-0-7603-5780-4

Library of Congress Cataloging-in-Publication Data

Names: Peterson, Chris, 1961- author.
Title: Bathroom ideas you can use: the latest designs, styles, fixtures,
  surfaces and remodeling tips / Chris Peterson.
Description: Updated edition. | Minneapolis, Minnesota: Cool Springs Press,
  2018.
Identifiers: LCCN 2017028169 | ISBN 9780760357804 (sc)
Subjects: LCSH: Bathrooms—Remodeling. | Interior decoration.
Classification: LCC TH4816.3.B37 P435 2018 | DDC 690/.42--dc23
LC record available at https://lccn.loc.gov/2017028169

Acquiring Editor: Mark Johanson
Project Manager: Nyle Vialet
Art Director: Brad Springer
Cover & Interior Design: Amy Sly

Printed in China

# Contents

# INTRODUCTION

This new edition of *Bathroom Ideas You Can Use* captures the latest ideas driving bathroom design. Those ideas aren't really about big changes, or eye-opening new technologies. They're more about small upgrades that increase how luxurious and stylish a home bathroom can be.

Take toilets for instance; toilet technology hasn't changed much since the first edition of this book came out. Heck, it hasn't changed much for a couple of decades. Little by little, toilets have become more efficient, able to flush more powerfully with ever decreasing amounts of water. But most homeowners won't notice those degree-by-degree efficiencies.

What they are likely to notice is the increasing profusion of toilet styles. From simple, barely-there, modern wall-mounted units, to elegant, almost poetic, unibody toilets, toilet looks have never been more varied. The variety of seat heights is a reflection of the trend toward more comfortable fixtures that can be adjusted to suit personal preference.

As convenient as the right toilet may be, the real decadence of a bathroom is all about showering and bathing. That's also where some of the most interesting bathroom innovations in recent times are coming to life. Technology keeps making inroads into our watery

**RUN A VISUAL THREAD THROUGH YOUR BATHROOM DESIGN TO TIE DECORATIVE ELEMENTS TOGETHER AND PROVIDE GRAPHIC LOGIC FOR THE EYE.** This clean, contemporary space incorporates an understated wood vanity, with solid surface countertop and marble backsplash. The elements are tied together with stunning gold-toned faucets, offering a scintillating combination of elegant form and eye-catching finish. That finish and form are echoed in the vanity door handles and towel bar, creating an engaging continuity in the look.

**PICK AN OPEN-SPOUT FAUCET FOR MAJOR VISUAL INTEREST.** This new style of faucet exposes part of the spout to create a unique and exciting faucet design. Although the style is available in widespread faucets, the wall-mounted version shown here really exploits the look and pairs perfectly with luxury wall tile and a marble vanity.

rituals, such as new showerheads that come equipped with Bluetooth speakers or fun, colored LED lights. Multihead showers—sometimes with more than one head on the same shower handle—are now, more than ever, an affordable luxury. Manufacturers far and wide are producing showerhead sets for just this purpose. Those manufacturers also continue to refine the shower enclosure, continuing the trend toward seamless design, with floating glass walls; integrated, all-in-one prefab enclosures; and curbless shower bases.

Prefer a bath? You're in luck; bathtub design is evolving as well. Manufacturers are going out of their way to accommodate all sizes of bathrooms. Freestanding tubs are becoming ever more popular for their adaptability and purely cool look, and deep soaking tubs remain favorites among these unattached models. Large, two-person jetted tubs are the pinnacle of bathing luxury. But you'll also find super-stylish variations for alcoves and drop-in locations. Not to mention the faucets and fixtures offered with new tubs can take basic features to the level of artwork.

Perhaps the biggest change in bathroom design these days is happening in the area of accessibility features, or what is known as *universal design* and *aging in place* (for the disabled and mobility-challenged elderly, respectively). What was only a few years ago a set of bland, function-only fixtures is now a dynamic area of bathroom design. Codes may dictate these features to be included in new and retrofit bathrooms—or in special situations for disabled users—but the market has demanded units that look less like they belong in an institution. Consequently, walk-in tubs are now so stylish that many younger and fully mobile people are including them as deep-soaking features that will be there when the homeowner eventually ages and becomes less mobile. Grab bars are another safety feature now offered in a spectacular range of colors, materials, and finishes.

All that translates to a menu of bathroom options each more beautiful than the last. Now there is no excuse not have the bathroom of your dreams that is a pure pleasure to use.

▶ **LET SHEEN REFLECT YOUR TASTE.** Contrasting surface sheens are a subtle and sophisticated way to spark a bathroom design. Not only does the unusual matte floor in this skinny bathroom really pop against the wealth of otherwise glossy surfaces, the high-gloss solid-surface ceiling adds an unusual and stunning element. All the surfaces are easy to keep clean and amplify the available light in the room.

▼ **OUTFIT A BATHROOM WITH A WALK-IN CLOSET.** The southwestern flair of this en suite bathroom and walk-in closet combo features a vanity and storage that not only match the cabinetry in the closet and dressing area but also look custom-made for the space. There is a vanity and matching storage furniture to suit any bathroom—even if the room has adobe walls and irregular stone pavers for a floor.

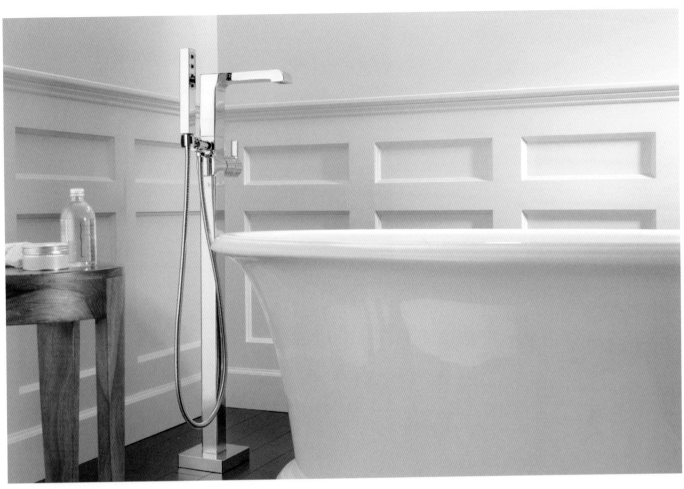

▲ **ACCENT YOUR UPSCALE FREESTANDING TUB WITH A DYNAMITE FAUCET.** Although modest faucets can be clipped right to the edge of a freestanding tubs (or installed in existing holes in the lip), a standalone tub faucet is your chance to add incredible flair to the appearance of the tub and the room at large. This squared-off model contrasts the curvy shape of the tub, and a barely-there spray head adds function and a little linear form to match the blocky design of the wainscoting in the room.

◄ **SINK FIXTURES INCORPORATED INTO A MIRROR OR WALL ARE NOVEL DESIGN DECISIONS.** Mounting sink fixtures through the mirror is an innovative and chic choice for bathrooms. The temperature controls are left on the vanity, while waterproof backsplash tiles create a clear border from countertop to wall. The matte black tile has a scintillating surface relief that invites the hand as well as the eye. Small details such as this can dial your bathroom design up a notch with a modest investment, regardless of the size of the room.

▶ **MATCH THE TOILET TO THE ROOM STYLE.** Reinforce your bathroom's design theme with your choice of toilets. The available selection of toilet styles is greater than ever before and, as shown here, includes some eye-catching shapes. This bathroom is equipped with both toilet and bidet, and as is done in almost every case, the two are a matched set. These modern-style fixtures are also low-flow, which is not only the socially responsible way to go, it's also mandated by many local, regional, and state ordinances.

▲ **WALL SCONCES EMIT SOFT AND SOOTHING LIGHT THAT IS PERFECT FOR BATHROOMS.** Choose lighting fixtures to not only serve the function, but also add a flashy form to the bathroom's design. Sconces, like this matched pair, are perfect for bringing a bit of drama into the room. Notice how the blown-glass shades on these units work perfectly with the wall paint color and also complement the handsome vanity-and-mirror combination. If you have your heart set on colorful light fixtures, it's a wise idea to bring paint and vanity finish samples with you when you go shopping.

▲ **CUSTOM TILE MAKES A SHOWER STUNNING.** Looking to impress in your bathroom? If you're willing to spend a bit more, you can't go wrong with a custom-tiled shower enclosure like the one shown here. Distinctive motif indicators like the arch used in this shower opening, the alcove shelf, and the wall detailing add even more flair. The mix of tile shapes, colors, and sizes is a sure way to keep the eye moving and interested. A bench makes this particular shower as luxurious to use as it is to look at.

**UPGRADE YOUR SHOWER TO TRANSFORM YOUR LIFE.** Create an unforgettable morning ritual by including multiple showerheads in your shower. The body sprayers shown here combine with an overhead rainwater showerhead to turn a simple shower into a hedonistic daily indulgence. A rail-mounted, handheld showerhead increases the adaptability of this shower and makes it even more luxurious. Low-flow versions (pictured here) let you enjoy the sumptuous experience knowing it's eco-friendly as well.

◄ **ACCENT WITH FINE FIXTURES.**
A concrete vanity top can be an impressive visual, solidly blocky with an unusual matte surface. But install a curvy, elegant widespread faucet set with a brushed nickel finish and add a visual counterpoint to the surface of the counter. The interaction between the two sets up a delightful visual tension and gives the faucet a lot of graphic power in the room—something a beautiful fixture like this deserves.

▼ **PURCHASE PREFAB FOR A CUSTOM LOOK WITHOUT THE PRICE TAG.** This shower enclosure isn't a custom tiling job; it's an all-in-one product, including everything you need for an Americans with Disabilities Act (ADA)-compliant, barrier-free luxury shower. The enclosure includes two wall ledges for hair- and body-care products, and deluxe multiple showerheads for an unrivaled shower experience. These days, luxury is almost always built into shower prefab products.

# NATURAL BATHROOM CLEANING SOLUTIONS

A lot of cleaners are on the market meant specifically for bathrooms. The problem with most of these is that they are loaded with chemicals. In some cases, very potent chemicals. Depending on the product you buy, bathroom cleaners can also be pricey. They are also unnecessary. The better bargains—and often, the more powerful cleaners—can be found in your kitchen cabinet.

• **GLASS CLEANER.** For a general cleaner that will remove smudges, streaks, and surface dirt from mirrors and windows, combine ¼ cup of ammonia with ½ gallon of hot water. To remove water spots from bathtub or shower enclosures, substitute vinegar for the ammonia. Do not combine other substances with ammonia; some, such as bleach, can mix with the ammonia to produce toxic gas. Acidic substances will neutralize the ammonia, zapping any cleaning power.

• **ABRASIVE CLEANER.** Combine equal parts borax, baking soda, and salt, and mix well. Sprinkle the mixture on the surface to be cleaned, and then moisten the mixture with a spray of water. Scrub until the surface is clean, and then rinse to remove the paste.

• **TOILET BOWL FRESHENER.** Sprinkle baking soda liberally around the bowl and then spritz with ½ cup (or more) of lemon juice. Let sit for 20 minutes or up to an hour before flushing.

• **DRAIN CLEANER.** This can be used to freshen drains and, done once a month, can head off clogs. Slowly sprinkle about 1 cup of baking soda down the drain, using a small amount of water to wash it into the pipes. Pour about ½ cup of vinegar slowly down the drain, and let the fizzing action clean out the pipes. After about 10 minutes, flush the drain with boiling water.

**REPEAT SHAPES FOR A SOOTHING, SUBTLE EFFECT.** Bathroom design details don't need to be ostentatious or over the top to make a big impact. This simple black-and-white bathroom is made more stylish with the addition of a frosted-glass divider at the foot of the tub, a simple black bathmat over an understated sisal rug, and unusual shelves that offer dynamic shapes and plenty of visual interest. All the fixtures are kept simple and white, and contemporary faucet fittings reinforce the room's uncomplicated—yet beautiful—aesthetic.

# BATHROOMS BY SIZE

Powder Rooms & Half Baths

Detached & Guest Bathrooms

Large & Master Baths

A bathroom's size determines to a great extent what decorative features work best in the room. In fact, when bathroom designs fail, it's often because the homeowner ignored the constraints of the room's dimensions. This is interior design 101, and ignoring the size of a bathroom when choosing a color scheme, fixtures,

furniture, and accents is a sure way to wind up with a less-than-satisfying look.

Half baths and powder rooms are usually not used every day and are the bathrooms most often seen by guests. Because of the small surface area and square footage, you can safely splurge in these rooms to make a decorative statement. You can also go a little wild with color schemes or wall coverings, because it won't take you a massive amount of effort to rectify if your visual experimentation goes awry.

Midsized bathrooms—the detached spaces that usually serve many people and including bathing facilities—are some of the more challenging to design, precisely because you most likely have to accommodate a variety of potential users, young to old, guests and residents. That's why these bathrooms often focus on stylish storage and attractive efficiency. But always keep in mind there simply is no excuse for sacrificing a bathroom's look to function. The two can always be married.

Master bedrooms, or large, expansive bathrooms that aren't attached to a bedroom, represent a chance to really indulge a sense of luxury. When you have the room (and budget), you can afford a decadently tiled shower enclosure with multiple heads next to an oversized jetted tub and his-and-her sinks. The possibilities become mind-boggling and it also becomes more important that the look meshes with the look of the master bedroom and the house itself.

This much is certain, though: regardless of the size of the bathroom you're looking to update, you'll find wonderful, useful ideas in this section.

**APPOINT POWDER ROOMS WITH SMALL FIXTURES TO INCREASE THE VISUAL SPACE.** As this photo clearly shows, you'll find fixtures, furnishings and fittings full of flair for even the most modest powder room space. The cylindrical vanity features a small amount of concealed storage, just right for the few essentials necessary in a tiny bathroom. Chic pendant lights hanging on each side of the understated mirror spice up the look of the room and illuminate what can often be a fairly shadowy space.

◀ **WARM UP A POWDER ROOM WITH WOOD.** The horizontal wood paneling gives this room a slightly eclectic, country feel. The informal design style is kept from being kitschy by the classic look of the pedestal sink and the elongated, unibody toilet. Those fixtures are restrained anchor points in a room design that includes a funky round mirror and casual wicker basket for towel storage.

▼ **SPLURGE ON MATERIALS FOR POWDER ROOMS.** The gray tile covering the floor and walls in this bathroom establishes a very sophisticated look, one made richer with a sleek wall-mounted sink and vanity and wall-mounted toilet. The wall-mount faucet reinforces the modern vibe, as do the elegant hanging pendants. The room includes a cool, water-conserving flush actuator on the wall, providing dual-flush capability.

▶ **CHOOSE A POWDER ROOM FAUCET CAREFULLY.**
The ideal small-bathroom sink fixture not only blends with the room's style, but it also embellishes the aesthetic. This modern faucet is the perfect powerful accent to a clean, contemporary powder room with a white porcelain sink and gray walls. Notice how the faucet echoes the finish of the mirror frame, and water glass and soap holders. Repetition of finishes and textures helps establish a sleek thread that can hold a small bathroom's design style together.

▼ **INSTITUTE CLASSIC LUXURY IN A SMALL POWDER ROOM.** Because you won't need to match bath, shower, and sink faucets, a powder room allows you to go a bit over the top with your fixture choices. It's also true that small design features carry a lot of weight in these tinier bathrooms. Here, the designer has used a classic luxury pairing of black and gold, with a stunning faucet that includes fine detailing and a mix of intriguing textures and shapes.

**PAIR COOL, NATURAL COLORS AND SYMMETRY FOR VISUALLY INTERESTING BATHROOMS THAT DON'T OVERWHELM THE EYE.**
The pale green on the walls of this small space bring to mind nature and are perfectly accented by the off-white trim. There is a calming effect to colors in green and blue families. The captivating color scheme here also moderates the busy wall decorations, providing the perfect foundation for the room's décor.

**SHOW OFF HALF BATHROOMS AND POWDER ROOMS WITH FINE FLOOR TREATMENTS.** More expensive flooring might not be practical in a larger, busier bathroom, but it's perfect here. This colonial-style half bath features lovely wood wainscoting and detailed casework, as well as a stunning oak floor. The light honey color of the floor and the unusual height of the wainscoting serve to raise the ceiling and increase the sense of space in the bathroom.

▲ **MATCH WALL EFFECTS TO FIXTURES FOR SUBTLE BEAUTY.** Sponging, rag-rolling, stippling and other effects are perfect for such a small, contained space, and they create visual excitement without overwhelming the room. Choose colors carefully to avoid jarring contrasts between the base and top coats and complement the fixtures and furniture in the room—as the brown paint on these walls complements the formal vanity and serves as the perfect backdrop for an ornate mirror frame.

◀ ▲ **USE TILE, RECESSED WINDOWS, MIRRORS, AND BASE MOLDING IN TANDEM TO ENHANCE A SMALL SPACE.** Contrary to conventional wisdom, multiple fixtures in the right dark colors can enhance a small space and actually make it seem larger. The colors in this two-tone paint scheme are separated by a band of tiles, a technique that works wonderfully no matter what size the room or what colors you use. Neutral colors tone down a busy aesthetic.

◀ **KEEP THE SMALLEST SPACES SIMPLE.** If your toilet and sink are positioned next to each other in a corner, use a small sink to avoid crowding someone sitting on the toilet. Always choose fixtures and position them with the space between kept firmly in mind. Notice that no storage or other furniture has been placed in the corner; leaving the space relatively free ensures easy movement between toilet and sink and creates more visual space as well. The choice of white walls and floor, with a basic decorative border of patterned tiles, visually opens up the room.

▲ **THINK OUTSIDE THE CONVENTIONAL BOX IN A GUEST BATHROOM.** Although chrome remains the most common finish for bathroom sink faucets, you don't have to follow the herd. Dark faucet finishes can add a tiny spot of drama and visual tension to the room, spicing up the design. If you decide to go in this direction, it's a good idea to use handles, knobs, toilet paper holders, or towel bars in the same finish, to prevent the faucet from looking like an accidental choice and an orphan of contrast.

▶ **KEEP YOUR COMMUNITY BATHROOM ORGANIZED TO AVOID VISUAL (AND REAL-LIFE) CHAOS.** Innovative storage solutions are always a welcome addition to any bathroom, but no more so than in a room that sees a lot of use from multiple people. It doesn't take much searching to find exactly the storage you need in prefab forms like this pullout vanity drawer featuring abundant small-item storage. A specialized storage feature like this can go a long way toward keeping you organized, saving time and headaches.

**SPLURGE ON THAT SPECIAL FIXTURE FOR A DEDICATED GUEST BATHROOM.** Any bathroom used almost exclusively by visitors to your house is the perfect opportunity to show off your sense of style. A one-of-a-kind feature such as the "blade" wall-mounted faucet and tray console sink in this room are ideal high-impact visuals. Notice the matching shelf and the asymmetrical wall composition that adds both visual excitement and a pleasing graphic element.

**LOW KEY WORKS IN GUEST BATHS.** Sometimes a subdued design provides the most welcoming comfort in a space used by many people, so don't hesitate to go low key in your guest bath. Here, a gold bathmat, towels, and other accents liven up the room's classic gray-and-white scheme. An oak hardwood floor provides an unexpected look underfoot, and crisp chrome accents and fixtures in the bath and shower provide an upscale polish.

### ▲ DESIGN TO THE ROOM'S AVAILABLE SPACE AND SHAPE.

Design a detached bathroom to optimize the space, getting as much as you can from the room. This long, narrow guest bathroom features a slim—but deep—soaking tub that offers a lot of luxury in a small footprint. Likewise, the glass walls of the shower enclosure are not only chic and afford maximum light penetration, they are also much thinner than a traditional wall, taking up far less space (both visually and physically). A narrow solid-surface vanity top with integral his-and-her sinks caps off a space-efficient and understated yet powerful bathroom design.

### ▶ NEO-ANGLES SAVE SPACE.

Add a shower to a bathroom that seems squeezed for space by using a neo-angle shower kit. These types of shower enclosures tuck into a corner and take up very little floor space, making them appropriate for even modestly sized guest baths. The unit here was built with a metal frame, but you can also find more modern-looking frameless neo-angle enclosures. You can build a neo-angle shower from scratch or turn to one of the many kits available that make the process easier and quicker—not to mention increasing your style choices.

**CHOOSE FIXTURES TO SUIT AVAILABLE SPACE.** Outfit an attic guest bath with space considerations in mind. This compact room features a tiny cabinet where the vanity would have gone, because there was no plumbing for a sink. The shower enclosure is positioned for maximum headroom, and the cabinet supplies just enough storage for the essentials (such as a back-up supply of toilet paper). Often, in guest bathrooms, you have to make the most of the space the architecture gives you.

**USE CURVED SHAPES FOR INFORMAL, YET EFFECTIVE, DESIGN.** This is especially true in detached bathrooms, which tend to feature low-key designs that verge on boring. This room includes an oval shape bathtub that buffers the wealth of lines and sharp angles in the room. Introducing round or oval shapes makes a room design seem less stiff and less formal and can—as this room clearly shows—make a bathroom appear more inviting.

▲ **TUB SURROUNDS ARE GREAT SOLUTIONS FOR GUEST BATHROOMS.** Turn to a three-piece tub surround for an easy, handsome surface treatment in a guest bathroom's bathtub shower. These solid panels are inexpensive and available in a wide range of colors and styles, from the very plain to the more ornate, such as the faux tile and ledges shown here. They are usually formed of fiberglass, polymers, or other synthetic materials, which means they are lightweight, waterproof, easy to install, and fairly durable. Choose versions with integral shelves, cubbies, or other features depending on how many people use the tub and shower.

▲ **MAKE A GUEST BATH BOTH MORE ACCESSIBLE AND MORE STYLISH BY ADDING A HANDSOME WALK-IN TUB ACCESSORIZED WITH SIMPLY CHIC FIXTURES.** This isn't your grandma's universal design tub; think of it as an easy-to-use deep soaking version with a door. Today's bathroom accessibility and aging-in-place features focus more on good looks than ever before. The sleek faucet, handles, and rinse head in this tub offer as much in the way of eye candy as they do in convenience.

◄ **SAVE SPACE WITH A BUILT-IN CORNER TUB.** Detached bathrooms can be squeezed for space, but that doesn't mean you have to downgrade the luxury. You can include a jetted tub with a useful built-in surround by tucking the structure into a corner. You can also install a standard apron tub with plain sides for even more space savings. In either case, the placement leaves the floor area clear and gives the room a more spacious feel.

◄ **EMPHASIZE SPACE AND SUBTLETY WITH MINIMAL FURNISHINGS AND ACCENTS.** There's no harm in keeping your bathroom design low key, especially in a smaller detached bath. Here, demure taupe ceramic tile ties together the tub and shower areas, without closing in the space as bolder, darker, or more dynamic tiles might have done. The chunky wood console base for the sink provides a modest amount of style and texture, but its open construction also helps the room appear more spacious. All in all, the combination of neutral colors and simple textures and lines makes this a handsome, if understated, bathroom.

▲ **EMPHASIZE OPENNESS WITH LIGHTING, FORM, AND FREE-STANDING FURNISHINGS.** Bring a guest bathroom to stunning life with a minimal, modern treatment. This room features an open floor plan as striking as it is unusual. A graceful freestanding tub with a sweeping form tops an eye-catching marble floor. The modern tigerwood vanity boasts an off-center sink with a sleek modern faucet. Although this is an extreme design style, in the right house, it would be a showstopper.

**BLEND STORAGE WHEN SPACE IS TIGHT.** Make the most of available space for a busy family bathroom with careful cabinetry selections. Ample storage has been introduced into this small bathroom with just the right mix of top and bottom cabinets, along with a corner unit. The cabinets were bought as a set, which is why they blend so well together. But they have the same detailing you'd find in custom cabinetry, including fine drawer molding and glass-front doors.

**MAKE A STRONG STATEMENT IN A GUEST BATH WITH A VIVID, DYNAMIC GRIDWORK SHOWER ENCLOSURE.** As nice as a sleek, frameless enclosure might be, it's now a common look that is the go-to for many homeowners and interior designers. Sometimes the most eye-catching thing you can do in a bathroom's décor is to buck the trend. Install a dramatic enclosure like the one shown here and you add a focal point that dominates a guest bath in a good way.

**ACCENTUATE ALCOVES WITH TILE.** Some vanities are too large to comfortably fit inside a guest or family bathroom but work well in the confined space of an alcove. By tiling around it, the cramped space is transformed into an eye-catching focal point. Here, the wood used for the adjacent storage cabinets matches the trim on the bath deck, and the combination of shelving and drawer space ensures that there is a place for everything that needs to be stored in this shared bathroom.

**GET BUSY IN THE DÉCOR FOR A MODEST GUEST BATH.** Traditional wisdom has it that intricate patterns crowd a small space and make the room seem smaller. But in a midsize bathroom, a mix of patterns and colors can add visual fireworks and continual interest. Here, two different colors of octagonal tile create a dynamic background that works surprisingly well with a black-and-white, whale-themed, vanity-column wall surface.

**REPEAT TEXTURES TO UNIFY A BATHROOM DESIGN.** Outfit a large, luxurious bathroom with a suite of matching cabinets to create a unified design and a fluid visual flow. The stylish raised-panel cabinetry here even matches the bathtub apron, and the abundant storage ensures that clutter will never be an issue. When choosing a suite of cabinets, consider bonus features such as the vanity desk shown here—extras that make the bathroom even more special.

**USE IDENTIFIABLE STYLES FOR EASY DÉCOR DECISIONS IN A LARGE BATHROOM.** A recognizable design style such as the Asian-inspired look in this room is perfect for a larger luxury bathroom. Once you've identified the style, each decision along the way becomes easier. The stepped platform with drop-in tub is a particularly effective use of the abundant space, giving the room a high-end bathhouse feel. Insightful use of a traditional toilet and fixtures with simple lines complement the rest of the design and let the standout elements, such as textured wall coverings, grab the lion's share of the attention.

▲ **KEEP COLOR SCHEMES CONSISTENT FOR VISUAL CONTINUITY IN LARGE BATHROOMS.** Limiting the number of colors, and using only neutral colors, gives this bathroom a calm air. Color schemes are especially important in larger bathrooms, where the color interactions play out more dramatically. The neutral scheme used here may be serene, but the room hardly lacks excitement. A wide range of neutral tones— from beige to almost black—and a dynamic mix of tile sizes, shapes, and configurations combine with stunning decorative elements to make a bathroom design that invites the visitor to linger.

▶ **DIVIDE LARGE ROOMS INTO FUNCTIONAL AREAS.** Where your bathroom is large enough, consider dividing it into separate functional areas. A divider wall in this room separates the bathing area from the sink and vanity. A large cabinet unit positioned in an alcove provides enough storage for clothes, making the sink area also a dressing area—another function that can be added to a large bathroom.

**RELY ON WINDOWS TO LIGHT LARGE BATHROOMS.** This light-soaked bathroom enjoys a wealth of open floor space; a wicker chaise longue creates an area for pure relaxation—a common designation for large, luxurious bathrooms. Add furniture to your spacious bathroom to add function. Notice that this room doesn't scrimp on style elsewhere either; pebbled tile covers the bath deck and shower surround, matching the yellow monochromatic color scheme.

**RESTRAIN FURNISHINGS IF DETAILS ARE YOUR FOCUS.** Don't be afraid to let one or two signature features dominate the design of your master bathroom. This bathroom is an example of how an otherwise sedate and restrained design can showcase a distinctive decorative element. The neutral color scheme and lack of detailing create a calm atmosphere, one that serves as a backdrop to an incredible stone wall surface behind the vanity and a pile of river rocks used as sculpture.

▲ **MAKE A MASTER BATH POP WITH SMALL ACCENTS.** The marble surfaces, black floor, and frameless shower may grab most of the attention in this room, but the essential icing on the cake is the accents. Bronze towel racks, handles, and light fixtures lend a counterpoint to all the white. Modern, linear faucets bring to mind Japanese bamboo waterspouts and add shiny chrome visual touchstones in the room.

◀ **DON'T BE AFRAID TO MIX AND MATCH DECORATIVE ELEMENTS FOR A MORE DARING LOOK IN A MASTER BATH.** An adventurous approach can work well for the larger and more personal space of a dedicated bathroom. The designer here used contrasts to drive the look and feel of the room. A crude, reclaimed wood vanity is paired with an ultra-smooth solid-color wall. The brushed-nickel finish of the elegant widespread faucet and sturdy vanity towel rack contrast the chrome of the light fixtures. And yet the entire aesthetic comes together because competing elements are used in balance to create a pleasing visual tension.

▶ **DIVIDE AND CONQUER WHERE YOU HAVE THE ROOM.** This stunning space has been glass-partitioned into an outer toilet and sink chamber, and a luxurious bath and shower wet room beyond. The one-piece toilet blends seamlessly with the off-white walls, and the sundrenched, angular tub and shower area. Green ceiling beams and a warm vanity softens the look just enough.

▼ **MAKE THE BATHING EXPERIENCE THE CENTERPIECE IN A MASTER BATH.** This master bath is all about spa-like decadence . . . and all about the stunning freestanding tub. The sheet vinyl floor provides a subtle but watertight foundation for the watery feature, and a simple, sophisticated tub faucet is positioned to allow unimpeded reclining either way in this deep-soaking beauty. When function meets a form this elegant, it's often the only design statement you need to make in the room.

**MAKE MAGIC IN A LARGE BATHROOM BY INSTALLING JUST THE RIGHT VANITY.** This sexy, curvy unit has a super-stylish art deco feel that spices up an incredibly sophisticated, upscale space. It also has abundant interior space for handily accessible storage. An understated but showy one-piece, square-tank commode provides counterpoint to the flow of the vanity, and the duo anchors a rich style that includes high-end marble, gray matte paint, and chrome sconces.

# SCINTILLATING SURFACES

Walls of Wow

Tile Style

Fantastic Floors

Eye-Catching Vanity Counters

**VARY WALL TEXTURES TO MAXIMIZE VISUAL INTEREST AND SET THE SPACE APART.** Striated wall tiles practically beg to be touched in this compact, yet well-outfitted bathroom. Those popping white shower tiles? Not tiles at all, but a prefab shower surround that just looks custom with its incorporated grab bars and elegant shower controls. The sleek and smooth U vanity adds even more textural variation.

The diversity of surface materials is one of the things that most separates the décor of a bathroom from the interior design of other rooms in the house. Whether it's the lustrous, hard elegance of a marble vanity counter and porcelain-tiled shower surround, or the warmer appeal of a textured vinyl floor and natural wood vanity, the mix-and-match possibilities are enough to make any homeowner's head spin.

Sorting through all those choices usually starts with cost. High-end Carrera marble can make your master bathroom look like a Roman senator's retreat, but it can also crush your credit card. If you want the appearance of stone on a budget, you may need to turn to the many available styles of quartz (some of which convincingly mimic marble veining) or go in an entirely different direction with something like a durable solid-surface material.

You'll also have to weigh any bathroom surface option against practical concerns. Consider seams. The more grout lines, joints, separations, and seams, the more potential for water infiltrating the underlying substrate of walls, floors, vanity tops, and tub platform frames. There's also the installation to be considered. Usually, the smaller the tile or number of pieces in a surface, the more work the installation (and potential expense) it will entail.

All that said, you'll not only find a staggering number of materials with which to clad walls, floors, shower enclosures, and countertops, you'll find even more looks among those materials than you could have imagined. Never fear. Enjoy the creative process of sifting through those options, and you're sure to find exactly the look you're after at a price you can afford.

**BLEND COLOR MAGICALLY WITH THE HELP OF THE RIGHT TILE.** As a general rule, use large-format tiles in large bathrooms and smaller tiles in smaller spaces. Of course, as this bathroom illustrates, design rules are meant to be broken. By isolating smaller mosaic tiles to specific areas—and using solid-surface panels for the greater area of the floor—the designer added huge visual interest and color to a clean, contemporary space. You can use vibrant mosaic tiles to define a specific area, even in a larger space, as long as sufficient negative space exists in the form of an unbroken surface.

**MIX TILE AND GLASS FOR DRAMATIC SURFACE TREATMENTS.** Consider metal tiles to make your bathroom walls the stars of the room. Metal-tiled surfaces offer unusual appearances that sometimes fool the eye but always intrigue the viewer. The tiles are as easy to clean as glass or ceramic tiles are and amplify light in useful and sometimes extraordinary ways (like the reflection in the countertop in this picture). Exploit the allure of a metal surface by using a single color tile, or mix and match with other sizes or finishes—or even intermingle metal with glass or ceramic tiles. The design possibilities are endless.

**CONNECT A FLOOR TREATMENT TO A WALL WITH TILE.** Intermingle tiled wall surfaces for stunning contrasts and complements. A row of green mosaic tiles has been run across the backsplash in this bathroom and further into a section of the shower wall that is tiled floor to ceiling with white subway tile. The classic shape and bright white color of the shower-wall tile helps make the small band of mosaic tile pop, and the interaction draws favorable attention to both surfaces.

**USE TILE TO FRAME AND HIGHLIGHT FEATURES.** Define the different areas of a bathroom with different tile treatments to give the eye easy cues to follow. In this Tuscan-style tiled bath, a vertical grid of brown tiles outlines the sitting area, while a chair-rail border of tiles separates sink from mirror and visually sets the sink area apart. Top and bottom borders of darker tile unify the areas where water is used. It's a fascinating look that makes visual sense.

**USE INSET TILES TO COMPLETE A GRAND SCHEME.** You can choose tile to create a very specific style in your bathroom. This room has been tiled for a formal, period-style look. Special, highly detailed border tiles called "listellos" capture plainer white and beige field tiles, with insets marking both the wall and bathtub. Gold accents in the form of a gilt mirror frame and faucets are the icing on the cake of a regal bathroom design that would be right at home in a palace.

# THE BATHROOM SURFACE CLEANING GUIDE

The nature of bathroom design means that many different surface materials are commonly incorporated into the room. Knowing what cleaner works best on which material can keep surfaces looking their best in this high-traffic space. The right cleaner and methods also ensure that bathroom surfaces last as long as they should.

- **QUARTZ.** An alluring material that comes in many different appearances, quartz generally only needs a swipe or two with a soft clean cloth and a mild warm water-and-soap solution. Need to remove something sticky? Try a plastic putty knife. The "don'ts" are actually more important with quartz surfaces. Don't use abrasive cleaners or any substance that is acidic (e.g., vinegar) or alkali (e.g., bleach). Do not wax or seal the surface. (When the wax or sealant wears off, it will leave the quartz looking dull.)

**A QUARTZ SURFACE** such as this wraparound vanity counter needs minimal care to look beautiful over time.

- **PORCELAIN.** Porcelain is a favorite in the bathroom. Sinks, tiles, toilets, and tubs are commonly porcelain. That's because the material is nonporous, shiny, stainless, and durable. Among porcelain fixtures, toilets require the most serious cleaning on a regular basis. An abrasive cleanser is a good choice for the toilet. Be sure to clean up under the rim to ensure water holes don't become clogged with debris, rust, or mold. To revive an older stained bowl, first clean it with a standard abrasive cleanser. Then soak toilet paper in vinegar and stuff the wet paper up under the rim of the bowl. Add 2 cups of vinegar to the water in the bowl. Let sit for at least 1 hour and then flush and clean again with an abrasive cleanser. You can clean porcelain sinks or tiles with a mild soap-and-warm water solution. Stuck-on gunk can be removed with a plastic putty knife.

- **CERAMIC TILE.** Like porcelain, glazed ceramic tile is nonporous and easy to keep clean. A simple wipe down is enough for most bathroom wall tile. Shower tile may require a bit more attention. For a periodic thorough cleaning, mix a solution of ½ cup of washing soda and ½ gallon hot water, and scrub the tile with a nylon scrubber. Remove mold and mildew with a spritz of white vinegar, followed with rinse of hot water (or use a spray of ½ cup hydrogen peroxide mixed with 1 cup hot water). Many home-cleaning professionals swear by a final rinse of club soda to really revive bathroom ceramic tile.

- **MARBLE.** It is one of most sumptuous materials you can use in a bathroom, but marble requires a bit of care to keep it looking as nice as possible. Try not to let any harsh chemicals or substances sit on the surface—including toothpaste or mouthwash. Never use acidic, caustic, or abrasive cleaners on marble. The best way to clean anything marble is with a marble cleaner. This includes floors, vanity tops, walls, and bath and shower surrounds.

- **SOLID-SURFACE MATERIALS.** Manufacturers of solid-surface countertops, sinks, and backsplashes recommended cleaning with warm water and a soft cloth to begin with. If the situation calls for more cleaning firepower, upgrade to warm, soapy water; an ammonia-based cleaner; or a cleaner meant specifically for solid-surface countertops. You can actually do more toward keeping the surfaces looking sharp by cleaning up any standing water immediately. The longer it stays on the surface, the more it will build up a stubborn film. Avoid any strong chemicals such as bleach, and heat sources such as curling irons.

- **GLASS.** Although several surfaces in your bathroom may be glass, they may not necessarily be treated as equals. Glass shower or tub doors are often the hardest to clean because of built-up soap scum or hard water deposits. Clean stubborn buildup with a spritz of vinegar, followed by a scrubbing with a paste made from equal parts white vinegar, baking soda, and table salt. Rinse, and the glass should sparkle. Glass tiles should be cleaned with a soap-based detergent mixed with warm water or ammonia-based window cleaner (check with the tile manufacturer). Glass vessel sinks should never be cleaned with an abrasive cleanser, but should be wiped down after every use; standing water is the enemy of the finish on most glass vessel sinks. Periodically wipe down the sink with a clean cloth moistened with a mild bleach solution.

- **METAL.** All except copper and stainless-steel tiles should be cleaned with a mild solution of dish soap and hot water. Clean copper and stainless steel with cleaners specifically for use on those metals.

- **VINYL.** This common flooring needs little in the way of attention. A mop dampened with warm water is usually all you'll need to clean a bathroom vinyl floor—always try to avoid any buildup from leftover chemical cleaner residue. If you need to clean stubborn dirt, use a soap meant for vinyl. Always use the right product for your vinyl—no-wax cleaners for modern no-wax vinyl surfaces and cleaners meant for a waxed surfaces on older vinyl floors.

**THE BRIGHT SPARKLING FIXTURES** in this bathroom need little more than a quick rubdown to stay shiny as new, but the marble needs a bit more care—mostly in avoiding substances or scrubbing that could degrade the extravagant appeal of the stone.

**GO LARGE TO FRAME FINE FIXTURES.** Amazing, large-format stone tiles line the walls and floor of this room, creating an incredible backdrop to everything else. The subtle putty color of the surfaces is a foil to the pristine white undermount sink and chrome gooseneck touch faucets. The simplicity of the sink and fixtures mirrors the simple surface and modest grout lines in the wall, but stands out from it enough to provide pleasing visual contrast. Not coincidentally, the wall and floors are also super easy to clean.

**LET ROUGH TEXTURES DEFINE YOUR MODERN BATHROOM.** The beautiful and shiny jetted alcove tub in this bathroom is surrounded by unpolished concrete walls. The contrast is fascinating and is made even more so by the satin-finish dark floor tiles that split the different between the liquid appeal of the tub and the raw, rough surface of the concrete.

**SELECT SOLID SURFACE FOR A THOROUGHLY MODERN AESTHETIC.**
The limited seams, slick, shiny façade and sophisticated
colors of solid-surface panels fairly scream modern design.
Add a wall-mounted sink and toilet, brushed nickel grab bars
and a concrete floor, and you create a cutting edge design
that could be a centerfold in a modern home magazine. The
panels are particularly apt in this bathroom, which is a wet
room with purely linear dimensions. Flat surfaces and the
need to prevent any moisture migration makes solid-surfaces
the perfect option for the room—even if they are a bit
difficult to install.

**COMPLEMENT LARGE TILES WITH SIMPLE FURNISHINGS.** Take a cue from designers and use large tiles in larger bathrooms. Not only do they look more appropriate in a spacious room, large tiles take less time and effort to install. If you're using a sizeable field of large tiles—like the wall behind this bathtub—consider color very carefully. Play it safe by using tiles with a minimal amount of color variation tile to tile.

**CHOOSE AND ORIENT TILES TO CREATE THE MOST VIVID PICTURE AND TO ACCOMMODATE THE SPACE.** Tiles of any sort are more expensive than paint, to both buy and install, so you might as well get maximum bang for your buck. Running contrary to the trend of using shiny tiles in a shower enclosure, the designer of this space used satin-finish, rectangular glass mosaics in varying earth tones. Unlike most tiles of this sort, the tiles in the shower were installed running vertically. The placement gives them the visual feel of falling water, which couldn't be more appropriate for the area they inhabit. The choice of colors also allows the sexy finish of the shower hardware to pop.

**EXPLOIT TILE COLOR POSSIBILITIES.** Create incredibly stunning bathroom walls by using tile in unique elegant colors, such as the luminescent green here, and combining the color with a patterned surface, such as the undulations on part of this vanity wall. The pattern leads the eye from side to side and breaks up what is a fairly restrained modern design. The undulating tile surface also produces highlights that change depending on where you are in the room and how the bathroom is lit. This sort of changeable design element creates an interactive and sophisticated bathroom.

**FRAME A MIRROR IN TILE.** Make a plain vanity mirror fancier—especially in a room with detailed tile work, such as this bathroom—by creating a frame with tile. The rounded-profile tile is ideal and looks just like a custom-made frame. You can use tiles to create mirror frames from subtle to funky, and because the exposure is so minimal, the frame tile does not necessarily need to match any tile you've used on the floor or walls. It's your chance to be a bit creative with your tile selection.

**SAMPLE TILE DESIGN BEFORE BUYING.** When you're shopping for a very special and unique border treatment for your bathroom walls, actually lay out the tiles so that you get a true sense of how they work together. Designs on paper won't give you an accurate idea of how different tile textures, shapes, and colors will combine. Laying the tiles out is also an easy way to quickly edit any design you've picked, interchanging the layout with tiles that are on hand.

**PORCELAIN OFFERS MAXIMUM VARIETY.** Porcelain tile is your go-to option for a hard, waterproof surface in a nearly unlimited range of colors, shapes and sizes. Tile manufacturers also produce versions with imprint textures, which provide a relief surface that is not only visually interesting but also slip resistant. The color of the tile goes all the way through and can't be scratched off. Some types of porcelain tile look like cut stone.

**METAL IS UNUSUAL, BUT DISTINCTIVE.** Willing to plunk down a bit more for your tiles? If so, you can consider a wall of stainless steel or other metal tiles. These offer one-of-a-kind appearances and are virtually indestructible. The tiles come in finishes from high-gloss polished, unpolished and several in between, as well as many different colors. Metal tiles are offered in all the standard shapes and sizes, which is why they are often used to accent ceramic-, stone-, or porcelain-tiled surfaces.

**CERAMIC SAVES MONEY.** Turn to ceramic tiles for a relatively inexpensive option with about the same design diversity as porcelain tiles. You'll find ceramic tiles that convincingly mimic stone surfaces for a fraction of the price. Textured varieties are used where slip resistance is needed. Ceramic tiles are also incredibly durable and can last decades in a bathroom (although the grout between tiles inevitably requires maintenance, cleaning, and sealing).

**GLASS GIVES GUSTO.** Pick glass tile where you want luminous colors. Glass bathroom tiles are usually backed with white latex so that the colors are fairly bright even when the tone itself is more subdued. Glass tile reflects light, making this a great option for smaller bathrooms or those that don't receive natural light. Colored glass tile is colored through and through, although gloss surfaces will show scratches—consequently, glass tile is usually not used in rough-and-tumble family baths that see a lot of traffic or use by children.

**STONE IS LAVISH.** Natural stone tiles offer you an incredible variety of looks and surface textures—some of the most luxurious and sophisticated in bathroom design. The price range for these tiles is equally as varied. Polished and sealed stone is preferable so that the stone doesn't absorb water and undermine the adhesive used to secure the tiles. Tiles with irregular surfaces are often best underfoot to prevent slips and falls. Stone tiles are excellent complements to other tiles when used over the span of a tiled surface or as a decorative border row.

**MOSAIC HAS MANY FACES.** Mosaic tiles remain a favorite of homeowners everywhere. Available in most materials, the tiles are small (generally no larger than 1 x 1 inch) and usually grouped on a mesh backing to allow for easier installation. Some mosaic tiles are crafted of individual tiles in figural or abstract designs and can be used to create a repetitive pattern or as a showcase insert in an otherwise solid-colored field of tiles. You can also find mosaics in unusual shapes, such as the hexagonal tiles shown here.

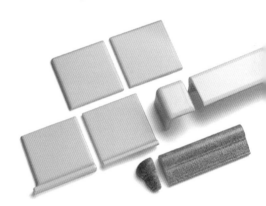

**CEMENT IS FOR CUSTOMIZATION.** Incorporate the unusual in your bathroom by using cement tiles. Cement tiles can be manufactured in just about any shape, size or configuration imaginable. The material can also be dyed a fantastic range of colors, and the surface can be stamped or impressed to create a regular or irregular surface pattern. Cement tiles are usually polished or otherwise sealed because water infiltration can compromise the structure of the tile.

**TRIM YOUR TILES.** Finish your tiled surfaces with trim tiles, specialty tiles designed to conceal the edges of field tile along the top or sides of a wall or vanity surface. These include bullnose tile, which is used to finish the edges of wall tiles that don't cover the complete wall surface, corner tiles to give a polished look at the corner of installations and many other specific tiles, such as chair or picture rail tiles. Some, such as border edge tile, can be pressed into service for interesting applications such as framing a mirror or window.

▲ **COMPLEMENT A ROLL-IN SHOWER WITH SOLID FLOORING.** This large, well-outfitted prefab shower enclosure comes complete with a flush drain that will take care of most of the water from the stylish showerheads. It's equipped with a beveled edge shower pan that allows a wheelchair user to access the enclosure with no problem. But that means some water will inevitably find its way out onto the floor. The vinyl sheet flooring ensures that no grout lines will soak up water, and the vinyl is entirely waterproof, so any splashes are no problem.

◄ **ADD WARMTH WITH HARDWOOD.** A wood floor provides a distinctive and unexpected look in a bathroom. The dark stain of this pecan floor adds a little drama to the otherwise bright white space. The floor itself is specially finished to resist moisture infiltration and damage from sun exposure. The wide plank format is an informal look. But regardless of format and stain, a wood floor provides warmth underfoot, and alternatives such as bamboo are increasingly being offered with finishes that allow them to be used in bathrooms.

**MIX TILE SIZE, COLOR, AND SHAPE TO ACCENTUATE YOUR FLOORS AND WALLS.** The porcelain tiles used throughout this lovely bathroom share similar finishes but exhibit an incredible amount of variety in their different shapes, sizes and colors. The border design on the floor is a classic bathroom style, and it's offset by witty faux wainscoting created with the help of long narrow tiles. The strips on the tub-surround tile tie that surface to the black border on the floor, helping unify all the surfaces in the space.

**TURN TO STONE FOR PURE DRAMA.**
The designer of this one-of-a-kind bathroom wasn't looking to make a tame statement. A true stone floor is ideal for the dark and brooding look, and unsealed stone soaks up splashes and drips from the tub or sink. If you choose to use stone floors for your bathroom, it's wise to contrast the look with stunning fixtures, such as the curvy contemporary toilet and slipper bathtub shown here. Both feature a bright white shiny finish that pops among the matte textures in the room, and add soft curves to an otherwise hard-edged design.

**WORK OUT COMPLEX TILE COMBINATIONS AND BORDER PLACEMENT ON PAPER FIRST.** If you're willing to go a little wild with tile, you can create a fun, funky, boldly colorful look that is all your own. This bathroom includes no less than seven different sizes and shapes of tile, and they have been combined in a high-energy pattern that is toned down somewhat through the use of cool blue colors throughout. No matter what, it's dynamic visual interest in action.

**STIMULATE THE EYES AND THE FEET WITH PEBBLE TILES.** Looking for something different in an informal bathroom floor? Try pebble tiles like the floor laid in this country-style bathroom. The tiles are actual cut pebbles laid flat and grouped on a mesh backing—each sheet is laid just as standard tiles are. The look is unique, and fun on the feet as well. You can find pebble tiles in the matte, uniform color of this floor, or in a range of muted colors, including blues, grays, and greens—even jet black.

**DIFFER FLOORING IN SMALL BATHROOMS TO DEFINE THE SPACE.** Where you have constructed a separate shower enclosure, differentiate key spaces in the room by differing the flooring between the shower and the main part of the bathroom. Here, a concrete floor in the bathroom proper is a very cool look and an easy-to-clean surface, but the use of mosaic glass tile in the shower enclosure defines it as separate from the rest of the room and gives the shower enclosure its own character.

**GO PREFAB TO SAVE ON SHOWER ENCLOSURES.** A molded, prefabricated tray base is the easiest, quickest, and least-expensive way to install a standalone shower enclosure. You can order prefab trays in a number of different sizes, shapes, and colors, and they can easily be matched to frameless walls, such as those shown here, to make for an easy-to-install stunner of a bathroom addition.

**USE SMALL TILES TO HIGHLIGHT FIXTURES.** Play it safe by following the conventional rule and use small tiles in smaller bathrooms and big tiles in larger spaces. The tiles here are a subdued gray that makes the floor and wall seem like a background canvas for the interesting fixtures, which include a contemporary wall-mounted sink and vanity and boxy cube lights over the mirror. One of the great things about tile is you can use it as a lovely background to other design elements or as showcase features in and of themselves.

▲ **MATCH WOOD FLOORS WITH OTHER NATURAL ELEMENTS.** Create a welcoming, informal appearance in your bathroom with a handsome wood floor. This tough oak floor has been finished to withstand the occasional splash of water from the tub, and it looks beautiful in a space that features a stunning freestanding bathtub with chunky wood-block "feet." All the elements combine to make this a simple and pleasing bathroom design.

▶ ▲ **MIX CLASSIC AND MODERN WITH CONCRETE AND WOOD.** Go with polished concrete floors for an extremely durable surface that screams modern design. This sleek floor is easy to clean and waterproof and is also fairly easy to install. However, it is a little cold on the feet during chillier months, a drawback you can deal with by setting down wood slats, as has been done in the shower area of this bathroom.

▶ **USE TILE TO CREATE SCENES.** You can lay a highly detailed floor such as this in your own bathroom using prearranged borders provided by the tile manufacturer. Retailers and manufacturers offer medallions, simple borders, special insets, and complete floor centerpieces like this wave design in mesh-backed, pre-fab sheets that are incredibly easy to lay. If you like the look of mosaic tiles, consider using them to their full potential in an intricate and splashy bathroom floor design.

# HOW TO CLEAN AND COLOR GROUT LINES

Transform older tiled surfaces in your bathroom without retiling. Thoroughly cleaning and recoloring your grout can make wall and floor tiles look brand new. This is an easy Saturday project that requires few tools, modest expense, and zero expertise. The process starts with a deep cleaning of the grout lines (a good idea to do on a regular basis in any case), followed by the application of a color that best complements the tile and room—a process that effectively seals the grout as well.

## Cleaning

• Always read the label of a grout-cleaning product closely. Most will etch unsealed tile, such as natural stone, and are consequently meant only for use with ceramic or porcelain tile.

• Wear gloves and work in small (3-foot-square) sections. Brush the cleaner onto the grout lines with a grout brush. Let it sit for 5 minutes, and scrub the grout again. Rinse with a damp sponge until all the cleaner has been removed. Let the tile and grout dry entirely, which may take up to 1 hour.

## Coloring

• Put a small amount of grout colorant in a plastic dish. Starting from the corner farthest from the door, begin coating the grout lines with colorant, using a foam applicator. Work in a grid about 3 feet square. Apply the colorant over the grout lines while trying to limit the amount of bleedover on the tiles.

• Use a damp sponge or damp clean towels to wipe the tiles after you've applied the colorant. Continue gently wiping them until you've removed all colorant from the tiles themselves. Note: You can also mist the tiles with water even after the colorant has dried, to wipe any remaining residue off the face of the tiles.

• Proceed to the next section of tile and repeat the process (you may need to coat the grout lines a second time to get satisfactory coverage or color).

• If the tiles are dull after you're finished, buff the face of the tiles with a scrub sponge, working diagonally to the grout lines.

**USE CONCRETE IN HIGH-TECH BATHROOMS.** Concrete seems like a natural choice for the bathroom, at once durable, water resistant, and inexpensive. However, concrete floors are most often used for high-tech or modern bathrooms, such as the one pictured here. The sleek X-trestle vanity and cool accessories set a cutting-edge style that the concrete surface fits right into. Polished concrete is the most popular choice, because the surface is entirely waterproof and complements a wider range of design styles. Keep in mind that concrete can be tinted every color of the rainbow and stamped with designs that not only make it look more interesting and unique, but increase the slip-resistance of the surface.

**USE BAMBOO FOR SUSTAINABLE, ECONOMICAL FLOORING.**
Turn to a different sort of floor—and an environmentally friendly choice—by laying bamboo strips or planks in your bathroom. Bamboo floors come in many different appearances depending on how they are manufactured. The grain may appear almost like a hardwood floor or closer and tighter like the floor shown here. The material can be left a light golden brown natural color or tinted in any number of shades and colors. No matter what type of bamboo floor you choose, though, you can rest easy knowing that it's a green choice—although it looks like wood, bamboo is actually a fast-growing grass that is totally sustainable.

**USE PLAIN TILES TO GROUND BUSY BATHROOMS.** Use large, plain tiles in a large bathroom when you want or need to provide a base for a busy design. The simple neutral tiles in this room are almost two square feet apiece, and the understated look provides some visual relief in a space with lots of lines, different textures, a mix of colors, and many different forms. Sometimes, a little plainness can go a long way in a bathroom design.

**MIX FLOOR TILES INTO THE WALL TO EXPAND SMALL BATHROOMS.** The most common application of mosaic tiles in a bathroom is to run the same tiles from the floor up to the wall. But mix it up for even more visual interest and to serve the needs of the space. In this relatively modest bathroom, the walls are a vibrant blue and white mosaic design, but the white mosaic tiles on the floor not only allow the walls to grab the attention, they also increase the visual size of the space, making a constrained room seem a little more spacious.

# Eye-catching Vanity Counters

● ○ ○ ○ ○ ○

▲ **MATCH NATURAL SURFACES TO NATURAL WALL TREATMENTS AND FLOORING.** Consider matching natural vanity materials to a natural vanity countertop in your bathroom. The Craftsman-style rough wood vanity here is perfectly paired with a slate counter. Stone vanity surfaces naturally complement wood vanities, especially those stained natural. Slate is just one of many alluring types of stone that could serve well in the bathroom.

▶ **MARRY COUNTERS TO OTHER SURFACES.** Mix and match your vanity counter successfully to the other surfaces in the room, and the look can be pure magic. Here, a super-colorful counter in polished volcanic stone supplies a burst of color in a bathroom with mirrored walls and white fixtures. It's a fun, dynamic, and exciting look in which the surfaces all support one another.

**MAKE A GLASS COUNTERTOP THE DOMINANT DESIGN FEATURE.** You can make a design statement with your vanity counter just as you would with your choice of materials for any of the other dominant surfaces in the space. Here, a cast-glass countertop provides a riveting visual focal point for the room. It offers an incredible surface that invites the brush of a finger and features a unique front edge relief. It's a one-of-a-kind surface that is also durable and easy to clean.

**▲ SHOUT LUXURY WITH REAL MARBLE.** The undisputed king among stone countertop options is marble, and white Carrara marble is the traditional look of upscale bathrooms around the globe. A countertop like this isn't inexpensive and it has to be professionally installed, but it can last the life of the house, the look never goes out of style, and it's incredibly durable. If you're going to the expense and commitment to install a vanity top like this, accent it with wall tiles such as the upscale versions shown on the left—a perfect match for the vanity top.

**▶ ENJOY THE UNIQUE APPEARANCE OF CONCRETE WITHOUT ALL THE MESS OF CONCRETE.** Quartz countertops are available in an incredible array of surface appearances, including the concrete look shown here (this particular variety comes in several colors). But the material is a whole lot easier to install, not to mention being just as durable and low-maintenance.

**SELECT STYLISH SIMPLICITY WITH A SOLID-SURFACE COUNTERTOP.** Solid-surface products come in a vast number of colors and are usually offered in a sheens ranging from matte to gloss—providing an amazing amount of design flexibility. One of the best features about this material is that the exposed edges are the same color and pattern as the top, so undermount sinks like the ones shown here are no problem. The countertops are also super easy to clean. Even if the surface gets scratched or damaged, you can usually buff out the defect with a minimum of time and effort.

**MATCH THE BACKSPLASH TO THE BATHROOM COUNTER FOR A PLEASING, SEAMLESS LOOK.** This is an especially important principle if you've decided to use a cool wall-mount faucet like the one here. Not only does this design technique ensure that both the counter and wall behind it are equally cleanable, it also visually ties the faucet to the vessel sink. The impression is that all the pieces are of a whole and coordinated with the décor.

**PAIR LUXURY WITH LUXURY.** A scintillating marble sink and counter should never be insulted by a cheap, low-end faucet. Instead, exploit the beauty of the material with a gold faucet that—just like marble—embodies extravagance and timeless style. This faucet even includes hardwood insets in the handles, and the craftsmanship is undeniably highbrow, just as the marble surface is.

# BEAUTIFUL STORAGE SPACES

Perfect Vanities

Handy Cabinets & Shelves

Showerheads get sleeker, new tile colors, shapes and finishes replace older styles, and toilet technology continues to evolve bit by bit. But one thing remains a constant in bathrooms across the country: the need for storage.

Bathrooms are inevitably some of the smallest spaces in the house, which is a problem because they are also some of the busiest, high-traffic rooms. Only you use your bedroom, but your whole family may be testing the capacity of that guest bath down the hall. Storing everything that needs to be stored to serve that traffic can be a daunting challenge.

The trick is to find places to store everything from towels, to extra toilet paper, to body-care products and appliances such as curling irons without disrupting the actual design of the bathroom. Maintaining the delicate balance between aesthetics and practicality means that finding the right bathroom storage requires a good deal of thought. Fortunately, manufacturers have done a lot of the thinking for you. They have developed flexible storage solutions adaptable to almost any bathroom.

If the options available on the marketplace don't meet your needs, you just need to exercise a little creativity—such as adding wine racks for towel storage, installing overdoor cabinets, or repurposing a spice-holder lazy Susan for your cosmetics. With a little thought and creativity, your bathroom design will shine, with a place for everything and everything in its place.

◄ **MATCH VANITY TO ROOM STYLE.** With so many styles, sizes, and types of vanities available, you should have no problem matching one to your particular bathroom design. The vanity in this room is a cool, linear design that suits the room's modern look, and the dark wood finish plays perfectly against the yellow accent wall. A side cabinet in the vanity supplies a nice amount of hidden storage.

**ADD A VANITY COMBINING STORAGE TYPES.** Choose a guest-bathroom vanity that has a variety of both open and concealed storage for an amazingly useful addition to the room. A unit such as the one shown here takes up modest space but includes both open shelves and concealed cabinet storage. This vanity provides almost all the storage that you would need in the room. The mix of storage types allows you to display high-style towels and attractive personal care products while hiding away more utilitarian objects such as toilet paper and general cleaning products.

○ ● ○ ○ ○ ○ ○

▲ **USE RETRACTABLE RACKS TO MAKE VANITIES MORE USEFUL.** Make any vanity even more useful with slide-out storage racks. These can hold all kinds of items, and the wire construction is easy to clean in the event of a spill (although you can find solid, slide-out drawers as well). Some vanities and bathroom cabinets come equipped with these types of storage features, but you can easily retrofit your existing undersink or cabinet areas with trays on runners like this one.

▶ ▲ **CHOOSE A VANITY WITH A MIX OF DRAWERS AND SHELVES IN SHARED BATHROOMS.** Always check the interior space carefully when considering which vanity to buy. A mix of drawers and open cabinet space is often the best solution for a shared bathroom, where many different items need to be stored. The option here, with the clean look of a pair of cabinet doors on the front of the vanity and a hidden drawer inside, offers a lot of flexibility in what you can store. Drawers, in particular, go a long way toward keeping odd-shaped bottles, jars and other containers in order.

▶ **USE WIDE VANITIES FOR TWO PEOPLE.** You can accommodate his-and-her sinks with abundant storage by using a single vanity meant specifically for two users, such as this one. Each sink has its own drawer and dedicated shelf, but the two units are complemented and attached with a central column of drawers that add a lot of storage and create a sharp look. Stainless steel feet are the icing on the cake for a handsome vanity that would work in many different bathroom designs.

**CUSTOMIZE VANITY CABINET STORAGE.** Make the most of any vanity by equipping it with specialized storage shelves that accommodate your particular needs. Door racks, a special corner shelf, and a tilt-out drawer on top all make this vanity more useful. Choose features like this in a new vanity or as add-ons to retrofit your existing unit, and you'll have taken a big step toward efficiently organizing your bathroom.

**MATE SINK STYLE WITH VANITY CONSTRUCTION.** Put some thought into the sink you marry with your vanity of choice. Here, a copper vessel sink looks perfect atop a bamboo vanity. The natural materials work great together, but the drawer really shows how suited they are for each other; a slot that divides the drawer allows room for the sink's drainpipe under the vanity's top surface.

**MATCH A PAIR OF MIRRORS TO A PAIR OF VANITIES.** His-and-her sinks are alluring when paired with his-and-her vanities. This twin setup illustrates just how attractive mirror-image sinks and vanities can be. The matching vanities host square vessel sinks and feature unusual corner handles on the drawers and cabinets, blending into an intriguing cross pattern. The mirrors follow the theme, and their off-center placement echoes the placement of the sinks.

▲ **CHOOSE A WALL-MOUNTED VANITY THAT INCLUDES TRAITS OF A TRADITIONAL VANITY.** Don't make the mistake of thinking you have to choose between the sleek appearance and open feel of a wall-mounted vanity and the storage you would expect of a traditional style. This unit provides a traditional appearance with loads of hidden and exposed storage, but in a form designed to increase visual space. The floor is left clear, you have storage to spare, and the style is worth writing home about!

◄▲ **COMBO VANITIES ARE STYLISH SPACE SAVERS.** Settle on a great solution for your half-bath by choosing a wall-mounted vanity and mirror combination. This handsome example shows how space-efficient a combination unit can be while still providing plenty of style. A sophisticated white vessel sink paired with a chic and simple faucet sit atop a dark wood unit featuring a single cabinet and tall, narrow mirror. The mirror serves any bathroom well, reflecting an image that includes torso and some lower body, and the entire unit fits in a space narrower than what a toilet would require.

◄ **LOOK FOR A VANITY WITH VARIED TYPES OF STORAGE.** Find a multifaceted vanity such as this and you may start to expand your notion of what should be stored in the bathroom. The central column of drawers provides the opportunity to store what might normally be kept in a bedroom or walk-in closet. This is especially true of a master bath, where the bulk of the dressing is done in the bathroom. You can keep jewelry or accessories in these drawers and free up room in your dresser or even use it to store abundant supplies such as bars of soap.

**STYLE VANITIES LIKE BEDROOM FURNITURE.** Bring the same classic style you might choose for a traditional bedroom suite into your bathroom by choosing an elegantly detailed wood vanity that derives its appearance from period-style furnishings. These two vanities are examples of sophisticated, traditional designs that exhibit all the marks of a fine cabinetmaker's skill and a style full of dignity and subtlety.

**ENSURE THE VANITY HAS THE DESIGN FIREPOWER TO VISUALLY SUPPORT SHOWCASE SINK AND FAUCETS.** Here, a gorgeous ebony vanity—that looks more like a high-end piece of bedroom furniture than a vanity—can more than hold its own with other features in the room. It boasts a blocky marble vessel sink and a chic single-handled faucet with an aqueduct-style spout. The faucet is a centerpiece, but the vanity provides plenty of interest on its own.

**ADD GLAMOUR WITH MIRRORED FRONTS.** Inject a touch of forties style with mirror fronts on the vanity. It's a small design touch that adds immeasurably to the look of the room and just spells fun. This vanity includes a detailed façade with mirrors in every panel. The white marble vanity top doesn't hurt the look either. A little flair in the vanity you choose can bring big design style to a bathroom, small or large.

# 5 INGENIOUS BATHROOM STORAGE SOLUTIONS

A constant in bathrooms everywhere is a shortage of storage. From cosmetics to hair-care products, to grooming equipment, shaving equipment, and washing accessories, there's just a lack of space in most bathrooms. Not to mention, you never have too many backup rolls of toilet paper or clean towels on hand.

This isn't just a matter of not having what you need, where you need it, when you need it. It also means there is perpetual clutter in the room—especially if the bathroom is regularly used by many people. Thank goodness that there are lots of simple, smart, and even fun storage solutions. Pick the ones that suit you, and get your bathroom organized and looking sharp.

### 1. Wall-Mount Wire Baskets.

Wire baskets come in a multitude of shapes and sizes, and can be spray painted any color of the rainbow. That means they're ideal for customizing and including in your bathroom décor. Once painted, use anchors and screws with flange washers to secure the baskets to the wall where you want them (use cardboard silhouettes of the baskets to play around with wall placement). The baskets make great containers for odd-sized jars, bottles, and even rolled towels. However, they're best when used with objects that have their own visual appeal.

### 2. Vanity Door Back.

The back (inside) of vanity or cabinet doors is actually prime storage real estate that is often overlooked. You'll find a wealth of specialized racks and holders meant to either hang from the top of the door, or be screwed right to the inside of the door. This type of storage combines accessibility and a hidden location that keeps visual clutter out of sight.

### 3. Door-Back Towel Storage.

Keeping wet and dry towels organized and out of the way is a central challenge in a busy bathroom. Answer that challenge by screwing large hooks to the back of the bathroom door, or attach short towel bars that can be used to hold dry or wet towels. In either case, make sure to install a doorstop or other door protector to stop the racks or hooks from damaging the wall when the door is flung open.

### 4. Shower "Shoe" Organizer.

Plastic hanging shoe caddies are widely available at retail and in catalogs, in a range of colors and designs. But any of these make wonderful waterproof storage for cleaning products such as shampoo or bottled soap. Simply hang the shoe organizer inside the shower from the curtain rod, and keep individual products in each shoe cubby.

### 5. Wine Rack Towel Storage.

Fun fact: A tightly rolled bath towel is about the same diameter as a bottle of wine. Take advantage of that odd coincidence by storing extra towels in your bathroom in a wine rack. The wonderful thing about wine racks is that they come in all kinds of materials and styles. You can hang a traditional wooden "honeycomb" from the wall, or use a standing metal wine rack for a more contemporary look where wall space is limited.

**VERTICALIZE YOUR VANITY FOR PERFECT SMALL-ITEM STORAGE.** Pullout vertical drawers are an option offered by many vanity manufacturers. As the ones shown here clearly illustrate, these storage nooks could not be handier. They are ideal for all manner of the small, loose items that seem to accumulate in a busy bathroom. The handy drawer puts cosmetics, small electronics, and much more within reach, but quickly out of sight when not in use.

**HIDE STORAGE IN WALL-HUNG UNITS.**
Look to wall-mounted cabinets for space-efficient storage. This example is especially effective, combining abundant storage space behind a flip-up mirrored front panel. It's a sleek design made even sleeker with interior lights and glass shelves. Find storage solutions that work as hard as possible in combining fabulous function with eye-catching form and details.

**USE FANCY TRIMWORK ON BATHROOM CABINETS.** Look for fine details on the storage cabinetry that you select to provide as much style as possible. Many of the storage units available at retail have a completely built-in look that will add something special to the appearance of any bathroom. Signs of skilled craftsmanship shout quality when included in bathroom storage, such as the crown molding top detail, mullioned windows, and raised-panel cabinet doors shown here.

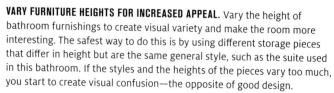

**VARY FURNITURE HEIGHTS FOR INCREASED APPEAL.** Vary the height of bathroom furnishings to create visual variety and make the room more interesting. The safest way to do this is by using different storage pieces that differ in height but are the same general style, such as the suite used in this bathroom. If the styles and the heights of the pieces vary too much, you start to create visual confusion—the opposite of good design.

**CONSERVE FLOOR SPACE WITH WALL-MOUNTED UNITS.** Add a wall-hung cabinet to a modest bathroom to create additional storage without taking up valuable floor space. The easiest way to integrate a wall-hung unit like this into the design is to match it to the style of the vanity and mirror. The pieces here all reflect a Shaker aesthetic, and small details such as the pulls and corner distressing convince the eye that these pieces are all part of a set—and an attractive set at that.

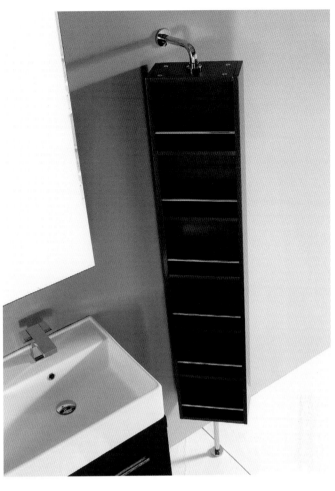

**SAVE SPACE WITH VERTICAL FIXTURES.** Follow the trend toward tall, narrow bathroom cabinets to make the most of available space in a small bathroom. This urbane unit is mounted between wall and floor but takes up a minimal footprint. The cabinet can be spun to either side for added convenience and access. The mirrored cabinet door adds to the vanity mirror, and adjustable shelves on the inside make the unit incredibly useful for storing just about anything you might need in the bathroom.

**MELD BATHROOM CABINETRY WITH THE VANITY FOR A PLEASING SEAMLESS LOOK.** There is a danger that storage cabinets can stick out like a sore thumb, especially if they are a radically different material, stain, or color than the main vanity in the bathroom. But as this bathroom set shows, it's easy to pair storage units—in this case, by running crown molding over the mirror frame and onto the top of the built cabinet. Extending the clean, white quartz vanity top onto the adjacent storage, and painting the cabinet-and-drawer tower the same color as the vanity (and using the same scalloped bottom design) also helps reinforce the impression.

**CREATE DESIGN CONTINUITY.** Create continuity in your bathroom's design by using coordinated storage pieces throughout the room. This suite of bathroom furnishings is a perfect example; the pleasing contemporary style mixing dark wood with chrome accents marks the wall-mounted vanity counter, the shelf underneath, and a vertical wall-mounted cabinet. The surface-mounted medicine cabinet complements the other pieces, and the total combination of storage ensures that everything has a place, regardless of its size or shape.

**HIDE A HAMPER IN YOUR STORAGE.**
Outfit a busy family bathroom with well-thought-out storage-space customizers to keep the room as shipshape as possible. This pullout, ventilated towel hamper is an incredibly useful feature for holding the wet towels in a busy bathroom while avoiding mold and odor problems. It gives everyone who uses the bathroom an easy place to throw towels when they're done, and it hides towels awaiting laundry, keeping the space looking neat at all times.

**STORE EVERYTHING IN A HUTCH.** You can turn to an all-in-one bathroom hutch to provide all the storage a bathroom could need. This unit is typical of the high-end, full-height units available, featuring an assortment of cabinet sizes and shapes, concealing both shelves and drawers. The styles on the market range from the traditional, like this unit, to much more modern and streamlined pieces.

**KEEP THE LOOK SLEEK WITH GLASS SHELVING.** Spruce up the look of any sink or toilet area with the addition of a nicely styled glass shelf. Glass shelves like this—sometimes called "vanity" shelves—provide a clean and airy appearance with little visual weight. This particular shelf is perfectly placed to hold personal care products used at the sink. It's also got a bit of style, boasting a chic chrome front rail and chrome mounts that match the faucet and the towel bar brackets. It's an extremely pulled-together look.

**USE THE WALL AS A BUILT-IN SHELF.** As this ultra-modern bathroom shows, you can literally build-in a shelving substitute. If you're tiling an entire wall, like the wall behind this bathtub, it's not hard to frame in a stepped knee wall in front of the main wall, creating a ledge that is much longer and stronger than most wall-mounted shelves. Although this ledge is used to hold towels and other light items, it could just as easily be used to store heavier things. It also functions as a wet wall to conceal the tub plumbing.

# BATHING IN STYLE

- Gorgeous Freestanding Bathtubs
- Gorgeous Alcove Bathtubs
- Gorgeous Corner Bathtubs
- Gorgeous Drop-In Bathtubs
- Walk-In Bathtubs
- Luxury Shower Enclosures

It seems like every day brings a new, stunning, elegant shape of bathtub or a new style of shower enclosure to the marketplace. The vast selection of tubs available range from the solid, chunky, and sturdy, to asymmetrical versions that seem to trick the eye, to sleek, streamlined models that look almost like they're in motion. Shower enclosures can, for their part, be built or installed in nearly any space with or without a pronounced curb.

All those shapes and sizes echo a boom in luxury features. More and more, even tubs rounding out the lower price points have multiple jets. Jetted tubs are that rare extravagance in a home: a rich person's luxury available to almost every homeowner. The pervasive influence of comfort and luxury has even bled into universal design walk-in tubs. Where once these units were bland and utilitarian, they now feature eye-catching designs, heaters, adjustable jets, touch controls, and other extras.

With showers, too, luxury has become commonplace. Manufacturers have made it simple to have a multihead showering experience, and the controls and hardware available act like jewelry around the neck of any shower enclosure.

With all those options at your disposal, it makes no sense to let the space define your bathtub choice. A freestanding tub can replace an alcove, a drop-in can replace a freestanding model, and a tub-and-shower unit can replace a tub alone. Shower enclosures can be created over just about any footprint—even the footprint of the whole bathroom. Different styles are largely interchangeable. Just measure carefully, and follow those measurements in your shopping excursions, and you're sure to find a tub or shower that is ideal for your bathroom.

**LEVERAGE SIMPLICITY FOR A COMFORTABLE BATH-AND-SHOWER EXPERIENCE THAT ADDS TO THE DÉCOR.** The basic, rectangular tub used in this bathroom not only provides a maximum amount of room for bathing, but it also accommodates a streamlined shower enclosure. The combination looks clean and welcoming, echoing the squared-off shape of the attractive toilet and the understated elements throughout the room.

**COLOR YOUR BATHTUB TO MATCH YOUR BATHROOM.** Add a little color to your bathroom by choosing a freestanding bathtub with a tinted body. A tub such as this brings plenty of seductive form to a room, but the muted color is a nice added touch that complements the room's color scheme and makes the showcase whirlpool tub even more of a standout. This particular tub is an interesting model, containing the motors and plumbing for the jets within the streamlined body—most whirlpool tubs are drop-in style, meant to be used with a larger enclosure. A tub like this allows for that same luxury without requiring the fuss of a custom-built platform.

▶ **MATCH A COPPER TUB TO WOOD FLOORS.** When you decide on a freestanding tub, you can pick from lots of unique looks. This tub is one example of the distinctive styles available. With an exterior surface clad in copper leaf and a deep porcelain interior, the tub would be right at home in a country-style bathroom or even a contemporary room.

▼ **SITE YOUR TUB ATOP UNEXPECTED FLOORING.** Do your tastes run to the unusual in tub finishes? Freestanding tubs may answer your desires because many are crafted in unusual materials. This tub, for instance, is brushed nickel and made from recycled materials. It's a completely unique look that seems right at home on a bed of river rocks. Don't limit yourself to white porcelain, because so many more options are available to the open-eyed tub shopper.

**SUSPEND YOUR TUB IN A STYLISH FRAME.** Go contemporary with an updated version of the traditional clawfoot tub. This bathtub is a drop-in unit suspended in an interesting wood frame with silver feet. It's a subtle and contemporary take on the classic footed tub, one that works well with a contemporary design scheme. Finding unusual and visually arresting alternatives to classic fixture designs is a great way to personalize a bathroom and make it a showcase.

**RETROFIT PERIOD FIXTURES TO NEWER TUBS.** You can even find colored versions like the clawfoot tub in this bathroom at high-end suppliers and firms that supply renovated period fixtures. You can also purchase an older tub from a salvage vendor and paint it whatever color suits the room. Just be sure to use special paint made specifically for cast iron or whatever material your tub is crafted from.

**CHOOSE FLARED FOR FLAIR.** Curved eggshell-shaped bathtubs are more common, but a flared tub like this one adds space and shape conducive to reclining. Like eggshell tubs, this one has a modest footprint and can be placed just about anywhere in the bathroom. It is perfect paired with a wall-mount tub faucet that intrudes on the bathing space as little as possible.

**MIX THE OLD WITH THE NEW.** You can choose a bathtub for its classic style, but always keep an eye out for modern conveniences and luxuries common to today's freestanding tubs. This clawfoot tub looks like it could have stepped right out of a hundred-year-old bathroom, except that it is equipped with levelers in each of the feet, and it's paired with a state-of-the-art freestanding faucet assembly that includes a handheld showerhead. Luxury and classic looks all in one package make for a pretty picture.

**SPOTLIGHT SHOWCASE TUBS.** Make a freestanding tub every bit the centerpiece that drop-in whirlpool tubs—with their substantial platforms and decks—often are. This tub has been situated in an alcove of its own with an impressive column of designer tiles rising up behind it. Detailed silver feet distinguish the fixture, and a rainwater head complements the tub faucet and completes what is surely the centerpiece of this bathroom.

**ELEVATE A BEAUTIFUL TUB.** When you've gone through the trouble of seeking out a very special tub—such as this deep pedestal tub with its unusual matte finish—consider showcasing it by putting it on its own stage. Here, the tub sits on an inlaid surface of stone that complements the stunning stacked flagstone wall behind the tub. Even the lights serve to emphasize the tub's simple yet engaging form.

# BATHTUB FACELIFT

Love that antique clawfoot tub, but is its deteriorated surface dragging down the rest of your new bathroom design? Don't sweat it—refinish it. Refinishing a tub requires a lot of elbow grease, but you'll save a lot of money over the cost of a quality replacement tub. A rewarding new tub surface starts with assessing whether the tub is really worth refinishing. Acrylic or cheaper tubs should probably be replaced. But if you want to save the unit you have, follow this easy process.

**1.** Clean the tub thoroughly with an abrasive cleaner. Follow by scrubbing with a lime-removal product. Thoroughly rinse the surface.

**2.** Use 400-grit wet sandpaper to sand the surface of the tub all over.

**3.** Remove all the caulk around the tub (for alcove tubs; skip this step for other types).

**4.** Mix the tub and tile refinishing paint (from a refinishing kit available at home centers and hardware stores). Paint the tub, moving the brush in one direction and applying a light coat.

**5.** Once the first coat is dry, repeat with a second coat, and then a third if necessary for complete coverage. Wait about an hour between coats. Recaulk as necessary once the final coat is completely dry.

**SHOWCASE UNIQUE TUBS.** The more distinctive the tub, the more you should consider making it a centerpiece of the room's design. Here, an antiqued copper pedestal tub has been placed in the middle of the room, resting on a handsome hardwood floor. The tub's finish fits right in with the floor's stain and makes the fixture the riveting visual star of the show.

**SET A STAGE FOR A SHOWPIECE TUB.** A stunning, beautiful, deep-soaking tub elevates the look of any room, but should be exalted as a design element and functional centerpiece of the room. One way to do that is to use beautiful, equally unique flooring like the artistic tile used in this bathroom. It not only provides a wonderful graphic element, but it is the perfect foil for the simple, oval freestanding tub.

▲ **CHOOSE A SEMI-FREESTANDING TUB FOR A UNIQUE LOOK AND POSITIONING IN A BATHROOM.** These tubs are a combination of alcove and freestanding, with the back meant to butt up against a wall. This means you don't have to run the plumbing you would for a full freestanding tub, but you don't require the walls you'd need for a true alcove tub. These can be wonderful tubs in a bathroom that doesn't have enough floor space to comfortably accommodate a freestanding model, but also doesn't have a natural tub enclosure.

▶ **SLIP INTO DECADENCE WITH A SLIPPER TUB.** The classic "slipper" shape of this tub makes for an incredibly relaxing, full-recline bathing experience. It's also a graceful look for any bathroom. Slipper tubs come in many forms, including the contemporary freestanding look here (which blends with a wide range of décor styles), pedestal tubs, and even clawfoot models. In all cases, it is one of the most comfortable shapes to bath in.

▲ **COMPLEMENT AN OPEN FLOOR PLAN WITH A SEMI-FREESTANDING TUB.** A big floor plan calls for a big "splashy" tub and this one answers the call. It features a side window and room for two bathers—including directional jets that are the height of luxury, and headrests that are the ultimate in bathing comfort. If you're an avid bather, a tub like this is well worth the investment and can be placed against any wall that has been plumbed.

◄ **PICK THE TUB THAT OPTIMIZES THE SPACE.** The choice of semi-freestanding model works well in this space, with an existing wall, but no alcove for an alcove tub. These types of tubs don't require a deck, and many—including the one shown here—come complete with their own fixtures and hardware, making them plug-and-play convenient. This tub's design is a bonus, because the projecting bowl shape provides extra bathing space, while not requiring more floor space.

▲ **TIE AN ALCOVE TUB TO THE REST OF THE ROOM WITH COORDINATED FIXTURES.** Here, the shape of the tub, toilet, and pedestal sink complement one another, but the real thread that ties the whole room together are the dark-patina fixtures, including tub faucet and showerhead, sink faucet, and towel racks. They provide dark, dramatic, visual stepping stones around the room that lead the eye through all the other decorative elements.

▶ **MATCH TUB SHAPE TO AVAILABLE SPACE.** Choose a bathtub shape to optimize the available space. Here, an oval tub fits neatly into a standard alcove, but because the front edge of the tub bulges out, the interior capacity of the tub is appreciably greater than normal. It's a great way to incorporate a soaking or whirlpool tub without having to structurally change your entire bathroom layout. The unibody design of this tub makes it easy to install in the space, alleviating the need to construct a separate deck.

**TRY AN UNCONVENTIONAL APPROACH FOR YOUR UPSCALE ALCOVE TUB.** A beautiful, deep soaking tub like this deserves something more than three blank walls. Butting it up against a large window provides a stunning view day or night (and blinds provide privacy when needed). The cement walls add drama to the location, and a windowsill-mounted tub faucet is an elegant and unexpected touch that caps a stunning look.

# Gorgeous Corner Bathtubs

▶ **CONSERVE ROOM WITH A CORNER TUB.** Saving space is perhaps the most compelling reason to choose a corner tub. The front arc of this unit allows for a much wider lane of travel through the room and can make a big difference in the small floor plan of most bathrooms. Of course, as this unit shows, the flowing shape of a corner bathtub is also appealing to the eye; most corner tubs are manufactured to maintain a large capacity even though they're configured for corner placement.

▼ **EXPLOIT A CORNER IN YOUR BATHROOM WITH AN OVER-THE-TOP, FUTURISTIC JETTED CORNER TUB.** What manufacturers used to consider an awkward fit is now an opportunity for luxury in confined quarters. As the tub here shows, corners are getting the glam treatment, with tubs molded to fit the corner and the bather, and add-ons such as integral fixtures and spout, and internal heaters.

▲ **GO ASYMMETRICAL FOR A DYNAMIC LOOK AND A MORE ACCOMMODATING BATH EXPERIENCE.** The tub here was formed to fit in the corner, but still maintains a maximum of bathing space inside. Situated in a high-end bathroom with special decorative wall surfacing, the tub more than holds its own. The modern, artsy ledge fixtures supplied with the tub are easily hooked up to an available water supply, and the tub itself is as easy to install as any corner model.

▶ **OPT FOR A CORNER TUB IN LONG, NARROW BATHROOMS.** As the unit here shows, corner tubs can make the most of available space in skinny rooms. However, if you are going to install a corner tub in a space where an alcove or freestanding model would normally go, help blend the unusual shape into the rest of the room by framing it in a complementing backdrop. The tile behind this tub carries on the color family in the rest of the room, creating a seamless transition between the room at large and the bathing area.

**USE TIERS IN YOUR DROP-IN.** Are you pining for ultimate luxury in your master bath? Where you have the room, indulge your inner hedonist with an over-the-top spa bath like this one. Featuring dozens of adjustable jets, molded back rests and body stalls, lights, and temperature controls, this tub provides a one-of-a-kind bathing experience. It also shines on the style front with a hardwood ledge and sleek faucet. A tub like this deserves to be the centerpiece around which a bathroom is designed, as is the case here. A backlit transparent wall, a row of plants, and custom step-up deck all give the bathtub top billing.

▲ **CHOOSE UNDERMOUNT TUBS FOR SUBTLER LOOKS.** If you aren't fond of the drop-in look, but you want to install a large whirlpool tub in your bathroom, you can turn to an undermount version such as this. The tub sits under a deck, just as an undermount sink does. This position minimizes the look of the tub's lip, and allows you to create a deck in any material that suits your design and tastes. The wood here has been finished top and bottom to ensure against moisture infiltration and match the wood steps to the soaking tub in the foreground.

◄ **EMBELLISH DECKS WITH BORDERS OF FINE TRIMWORK OR STONE.** Take the opportunity of building a surround for your drop-in whirlpool bathtub to create a unique, scene-setting feature. This tub has been framed in an enclosure that includes a river-rock border inside the tub's deck. It's a naturalistic look that complements the wood deck and the plants used in the room, and it gives the bather the sense of dipping into a serene stream. Special, innovative features such as this give you an opportunity to put your fingerprints on a bathroom design.

▲ **SELECT AN OVAL DROP-IN TUB FOR AN ENTIRELY DIFFERENT LOOK, ONE THAT CAN SERVE AS THE CENTERPIECE OF A DYNAMIC BATHROOM DESIGN.** Most drop-ins are rectangular because the shape lends itself to easy deck construction. But if you're willing to spend a little more, you can create a one-of-kind surrounding structure that frames the tub in an undeniably stunning way. The bent wood surface around this tub seems to defy physics, and the graduated lip of the bathtub makes for an elegant transition to the interior.

▶ **MAGNIFY MODEST WITH A TIDY DROP-IN TUB.** Your bathroom doesn't have to be gigantic or opulent to benefit from a nifty drop-in bathtub. The supporting structure here has been crafted to match the wood vanity and has been given a bit of flair with hidden LED base lighting and high-end faucet and showerhead set to match the sink's faucet. It's a sleek, subtle look, but one that can give any freestanding tub a run for its money.

**MAXIMIZE SOPHISTICATION WITH A TUB FEATURING A FINELY DETAILED RIM.** The lip of most drop-in tubs is simply meant to hold the tub in place on the supporting structure. But that doesn't have to be the case. This tub has an elegantly molded lip that sits 4 inches above the deck surface. In keeping with the chic style of the tub, the deck and surround are just as detailed and upscale. A chandelier and glass-and-chrome table complete the picture of an incredibly timeless bathroom look.

▲ **MAKE THE DROP-IN THE CENTERPIECE.** Create an incredibly inviting scene in your master bathroom by positioning a whirlpool tub as the centerpiece of the room. The drop-in unit dominates this lovely bathroom; the stylish tiled surround contains the heater and motor elements for the tub. The tub itself features both air and water jets, a range of settings, interior colored lights, and a specially molded shape to cradle the bather's body in ultimate luxury. Add a tub like this to your bathroom and you may just forget you don't live at a luxury spa.

▶ **MAKE A DROP-IN TUB WET-ROOM SAFE.** The deck of a deep drop-in tub is likely to shed a lot of water as bathers get in and out of the tub, or jets splash water around. You can ensure the integrity of tiled floor and deck by draining off any excess water in a sleek, barrier-free linear drain. These types of drains blend right into the room and sit flush with the floor. As an added bonus, the companies that produce them offer several styles of grille design, which can add a modest decorative element to your drain. In any case, it's insurance against water infiltration.

**REDEFINE BATHTUB STYLE WITH A MODEL THAT SPLITS THE DIFFERENCE BETWEEN A DROP-IN AND A FREESTANDING UNIT.** This stylish bathtub includes the small footprint and easy positioning of a freestanding tub, with the handy deck space of a drop-in. The result is an eye-catching look that serves the bather's every need, with a place for candles, drinks, or hair-care products. The bold, streamlined appearance complements the rest of the room.

**TRY OUT YOUR WALK-IN TUB BEFORE BUYING.** The interior of most walk-in tubs is surprisingly spacious and built for comfort, but you want to make sure that the unit suits your height, body type, and arm length. You should be able to reach all the controls easily and support yourself on the grab bars or safety handles in the tub. You should also make sure that opening and closing the door is easy and comfortable, and that getting in and out of the tub is no problem.

**TRIP THE LIGHT FANTASTIC.** Walk-in tubs, like many of their freestanding and even alcove cousins, are increasingly outfitted with colored lights that can be changed to different hues. The lights are more than aesthetic features; they are part of a health practice known as chromatherapy and are chosen for the effects the light color has on physical, mental, and emotional health and well-being. But there's no getting around the fact that they also make for a more beautiful bathing experience.

# BATHROOM ACCESSIBILITY STRATEGIES

A walk-in tub can be a key part to an accessible bathroom as defined by the Americans With Disabilities Act and the precepts of universal design. Whether you're creating a bathroom to be used by a disabled person, or just planning ahead with aging in place features, here are some considerations beyond the walk-in tub.

- **NONSLIP FLOOR.** This is an easy element to overlook, but many common bathroom flooring options are actually quite slippery, especially when wet. This extends to a shower enclosure or the floor of any tub, which should be lined with slip-resistant strips.

- **DOORWAY WIDTHS.** If you or any member of the home must use a walker or a wheelchair, you will most likely need to widen the doorway to allow easy access to the room. The doorway should be at least 34 inches, and preferably 36 inches wide to allow for a wheelchair. It's best to leave the entrance to a shower enclosure open, without a door. You can use a rubber dam to contain water as necessary.

- **RAISE THE SINK.** If a wheelchair-bound person will be using the bathroom, install a sink without a vanity, higher than normal. Wheelchair users will find sinks mounted 30 to 34 inches above the floor (bottom surface of the sink) most accessible.

- **TOILET HEIGHT.** Both disabled users and those with mobility issues will have an easier time using a toilet with a seat 2 to 3 inches higher than normal—usually around 18 inches. You can buy seat extenders to retrofit your existing toilet with a higher seat.

**PICK A TUB THAT HELPS THE BATHER.** Special-access tubs with swing-in doors are your best friend when designing a bathroom to accommodate users with limited mobility. These tubs are built with special seating that is easy to get in and out of and a door that seals perfectly to prevent water from leaking out. The tubs are perfect for the elderly or people with mobility problems, and the small footprint ensures that they can easily fit into most bathroom floor plans.

**OPT FOR A WALK-IN TUB DOOR STYLE THAT SUITS YOU.** This tub features a bypass door, in contrast to the more common "open in" door. In either case, the door securely seals against water leakage. This particular tub also includes a padded headrest and side-mount fixtures that could be more convenient for smaller people or those with shorter arms. Make sure the features of any tub you buy suit the way you prefer to bathe.

**ENRICH SHOWERING WITH A LARGE ENCLOSURE.** Exploit large bathroom spaces and make showering more luxurious by expanding the shower enclosure to fill an available open area. The large footprint of a shower such as this makes the morning (or evening) wash-down an unrivaled pleasure, and the combination of stone mosaic and large square tiles is simply jaw-dropping. Adding a bench is almost a must in a large shower, and you can build one in as the designer did here or add a waterproof portable shower stool or bench.

**BLEND AN ENCLOSURE INTO THE ROOM'S STYLE.** Make sure your shower enclosure design is appropriate to the overall bathroom style. Although it's tempting to view the enclosure as a chance for design fireworks in the bathroom, sometimes it's wise to be more subdued. The elegant, restrained, light, and airy look of this room called for an enclosure that blends in rather than stands out. The frameless glass doors are perfect for the light-filled space, and the shower faucet matches the bidet and vanity faucets. It's a perfectly unified design that's pleasing to the eye.

**INSTALL EDGE DRAINS TO INCREASE COMFORT.** Always try to minimize the impact of the drain on how comfortable the shower is to stand in. Center drains are the easiest to install, but they can make for a canted floor that is uncomfortable over the course of long, steamy showers—and who wants to take a short shower? This drain system runs along the edge of the floor, and needs only a slight gradient to effectively drain off shower water. It's a streamlined and sophisticated design decision.

**USE IDENTICAL BATHROOM SURFACES IN YOUR SHOWER ENCLOSURE.** Consider replicating stunning surfaces used elsewhere in the bathroom in your shower enclosure. The stone tiles used for the floor in this bathroom were also used as a tub surround and then run into and up the walls of the shower enclosure. Not only is the material inherently spectacular, but using it in this way also creates incredible visual continuity that ties together the entire bathroom design. Note that the larger tiles have been used throughout; large tiles look more appropriate in large bathrooms than smaller sizes would.

▲ **DON'T LET AVAILABLE SPACE LIMIT YOUR LUXURY SHOWER OPTIONS.** These days, it is relatively easy to install a shower enclosure in place of an existing tub or just at one end of a long, thin bathroom. That's because all the parts are offered as prefab elements. The enclosure, base, and fixtures shown here are offered as a package. A rolling bypass door adds a distinctively upscale element to what is a fairly simple shower enclosure that looks anything but.

▶ **REINFORCE MODERN OR CONTEMPORARY ROOM DESIGNS WITH FRAMELESS SHOWER PARTITIONS.** Frameless shower enclosure walls and doors are a clean, popular look. The barriers are sleek, making them ideal for the streamlined aesthetic of a modern bathroom, or the simple linear perspective of contemporary interiors. Manufacturers have responded to the popularity of this look, which is why it's easy to find a source for panels even in custom sizes and accompanying hardware in different designs and finishes.

**SIMPLIFY FOR A CALMING EFFECT.** Nothing says you need to make a big bang with your shower enclosure. Sometimes, simpler is better. The solid blue mosaic tile covering the walls and floor of this shower stall give it a calm, lovely aspect. The tile was also easier to install in straight lines and right angles than it would have been on curving surfaces or to execute a highly detailed tile pattern. The look is plain but beautiful and low key.

**ACCOMMODATE A TIGHT FLOOR PLAN WITH A CORNER SHOWER ENCLOSURE.** Build in a corner shower to exploit otherwise dead floor space, and create a luxury element in a tight fit. This corner shower is fluidly blended, sharing both the mosaic floor tile and the green brick wall tile. Frameless, clear glass walls ensure the space remains visually open and airy, and that natural light makes its way into the shower.

Although linear drains are all made to sit flush with the surrounding floor surface, the concealed drain tray underneath the grill is one of many different types, so that the installation can adapt to any existing drain or plumbing setup.

**STANDARD CENTER DRAIN WITH SQUARE GRILL**

**FIXED-FLANGE DRAIN**

**SIDE-OUTLET DRAIN**

**FIXED-LENGTH DRAIN CONNECTION**

**SITE-SIZABLE DRAIN**

**USE A LINEAR DRAIN TO KEEP WATER WHERE YOU WANT IT.** The increasing popularity of sleek, curbless shower enclosures requires a drain solution that is innovative and atypical. Linear drains are installed flush with the floor, with the floor slanted very slightly toward the drain. Although these drains are installed for very important and pragmatic reasons, manufacturers have taken the opportunity to create a new visual element by varying the grill designs. The standardized slots shown here represent just one of many decorative grill patterns.

**ADD PIZZAZZ AND USABLE SPACE WITH BUILT-IN LEDGE ALCOVES.** Make any shower enclosure easier to use by adding cutouts when constructing the enclosure. This particular shelf alcove is even more interesting in that the shower control has been located inside. The ledge is useful for holding soap, loofahs, other sundries, or just decorative touches such as the seashells on display in this shower. Cutouts are typically tiled, not only to match the enclosure's walls, but also to prevent water infiltration.

**SELECT STURDY BYPASS DOORS, FOR A STYLISH AND SECURE SHOWER ENCLOSURE.** Sometimes, a clean, simple, and traditional look is best. In a stylish, but low-key bathroom such as this, there was no need for an over-the-top shower enclosure. The squared-off vessel sink with luxury faucet, subtly styled toilet, and wall-mounted vanity provide all the visual excitement needed in the space. A white shower enclosure with built-in shelves and a rain showerhead stay true to the calm, understated nature of the room's design, as do the simple doors.

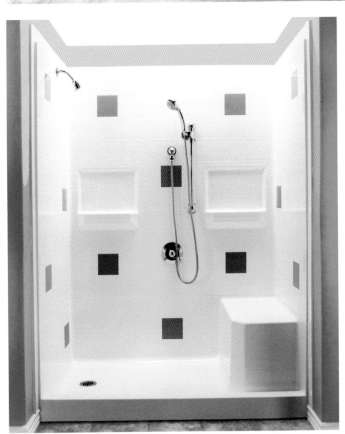

**BALANCE BUDGET AND DESIGN WITH A PREFAB SHOWER ENCLOSURE.** Not so long ago, prefab shower surrounds were flimsy and drab, with no flair or customization available. Those days are gone. Now, you can choose from a wide array of exciting and attractive design options, with many including tiled sections, integral grab bars, and even incorporated shower bars, multiple heads, high-end controls, and other features.

○ ○ ○ ○ ○ ○ ○ ● ○ ○ ○ ○ ○

▶ **CHOOSE ENCLOSURES WITH A BIT OF FLAIR.** The two prefab shower enclosure closeups shown here are examples of the details many manufacturers now offer. The durable, rugged surface of the enclosure has been embellished with bands of beautiful glass tiles. Simple details like this can go a long way toward dressing up any shower, and the options don't break the bank. Plus, they are a whole lot easier than tiling an entire shower surround.

▼ **GO CURBLESS FOR MAXIMUM ACCESSIBILITY.** Want everyone in the house—even those with mobility issues—to have access to your new shower enclosure? Install a curbless enclosure like the one here. Not only does this prefab unit not have a curb, it has a beveled lip to make wheelchair access easy. This isn't just a matter of accommodating a disabled family member; enclosures with these types of features are a way to ensure your bathroom is every bit as accessible as you age. These features head off trips and falls—some of the most common accidents the elderly experience.

**SCREAM "SUPER SLEEK" WITH A FRAMELESS GLASS ENCLOSURE.** It's hard to go wrong when you craft your shower enclosure with frameless glass panels. These are fairly easy to install, sexy to behold, and suit just about any style of bathroom. You can also find a fantastic range of prefab sizes to accommodate shower stalls large and small. And where a solid-wall enclosure might block light coming into the room, a glass cube allows for maximum light penetration.

**MAKE A 360-DEGREE SHOWER CURTAIN A SHOWER ENCLOSURE.** Who says a shower enclosure has to be a freestanding, separate construction? In keeping with the period look of this footed tub, the showerhead is run up from the Victorian-style faucet fixture with a period-appropriate shower curtain ring attached. The shower includes a luxury head with porcelain lip and a separate handheld head with its own diverter controls. It's a lot of shower luxury in a small amount of space, and keeps the distinctive look of the room in perfect order.

**BRIGHTEN A LUXURY SHOWER ENCLOSURE WITH SOME COLORED LIGHT.** LED technology means that you can find shower and bathroom lights in multicolored versions, and even in showerheads! A fun blue light like the one used in this shower adds an interesting element to the morning shower and the color can be changed at a whim. There is also a growing body of evidence that the right light can affect your mental and physical state—part of a practice called *chromatherapy*.

**KEEP A CONTINUITY OF FLOORING.** Want a sleek look that is easier to install? Use the same flooring for both the bathroom at large and the shower enclosure. The best way to do that is to install a linear drain. The drain sits flush with the floor, and the base can easily be installed at the same time the entire floor is. Linear drains also visually complement upscale flooring, such as the marble tile used here. The look works best with large-format tiles or planks, but a linear drain can also easily blend in with the right mosaic floor.

**SEPARATE SHOWER AND BATH FIXTURES FOR AN INNOVATIVE, INTRIGUING, AND APPEALING LOOK.** The elegant bathtub faucet here, with a period telephone cradle rinse head, could easily have been outfitted with a shower extension. Instead, the showerhead plumbing extends from the wall, out of a column of decorative tile. The design is unique but totally in keeping with the fine, fussy detailing throughout the space, a room embellished with ornamented sconces and fluted pedestal sink legs.

**◄ REDUCE YOUR SHOWER ENCLOSURE CLEANUP WITH A SIMPLE SQUEEGEE.** This stylish squeegee and hanger are meant specifically for use in upscale shower enclosures and they look the part. But the real beauty of this shower accent is its pragmatic appeal. Take a minute after showering to squeegee off glass doors, dividers, and tile, and you prevent any soap scum or lime buildup on the surface, making cleaning the shower a breeze whenever you do it.

**▼ DO AWAY WITH A SHOWER ENCLOSURE ALTOGETHER BY CREATING A WELL-TILED WET ROOM.** You may think you need a glass shower enclosure, but it would have only cramped this space and interrupted the visual appeal in the bathroom. The many different types of tile are all waterproof, as are all the fixtures and surfaces in the room. A central drain ensures the water goes where it is supposed to, and the open floor plan is kept beautifully intact. Wet rooms aren't for every situation, but they can be excellent solutions where you want to optimize absolutely every inch in a bathroom.

# SUPERB FIXTURES

Fashionable Toilets & Bidets

Stunning Sink Colors

Sleek Drop-In Sinks

Understated Undermount Sinks

Gravity-Defying Wall-Mount Sinks

Stately Pedestal & Vessel Sinks

A bathroom or powder room may or may not have a bathtub, and it may or may not have a shower. But every size and type of bathroom has at least one sink, and at least a toilet. Some even have double sinks and perhaps a bidet.

That's because these functional fixtures are the heart of the bathroom's function. Thank goodness their practicality doesn't stop these ever-present fixtures from looking great. Where toilets were once uninspired, simple, usable thrones, you can now select from a wide range of sizes, shapes, and styles. Sinks are even more diverse. Not only are more sink forms available now than ever before, but the variety of materials of which sinks are made has never been greater.

Placement is yet another variable. Sinks can sit atop a vanity, be the entire top of a vanity, come with their own support, or can even be mounted by themselves on the wall. Where toilets are always porcelain, you can find sinks in solid-surface materials, marble, glass, and even metals.

All that variety means the sink becomes the wild card in most bathrooms. Reinforce the decorative style with your choice of toilet—and select one that is comfortable to use—then choose a sink that feeds your sense of panache.

**LET THE MANUFACTURER COORDINATE YOUR BATHROOM.** The elegant toilet, sink, and bathtub in this sparkling white room are part of a suite, a family of fixtures. The wonderful thing about an upscale suite such as this is that the similarities are subtle—rounded corners, soft edges, and flowing lines here—so each piece stands on its own merit but also blends perfectly. In truth, any one of these fixtures could easily live in its own bathroom design, but they make the most powerful statement used together.

**GO DEMURE WITH A WALL-MOUNTED TOILET.** Wall-mounted toilets have become popular in recent years because they minimalize the visual impact of a fixture many people do not want to showcase. They also allow for customized toilet height to suit the homeowner. In any case, the streamlined form of wall-mounted toilets is a pleasing, subtle visual. It might be the perfect choice for your bathroom renovation, especially if you're instituting a modern or contemporary design as in this room, with understated, large-format tiles and a wall-mounted vanity.

# ROUND OR OVAL? THE GREAT TOILET SHAPE DEBATE

There has never been a bigger diversity of toilet styles and types. You can wall mount a sleek tankless unit for a modern appearance and completely customized seating height, or go traditional with a two-piece, porcelain, water-saving throne. But all toilets can be divided by seat shape: round or elongated (oval).

Round toilets save space—from the wall to the front edge of an elongated toilet can be as much as 31 inches, while round toilets will measure no more than 28 inches. In a small, modest bathroom—especially the narrow footprint common to so many bathrooms—a few inches can make a big difference. That said, elongated seats are more comfortable for most people, which is why they're more popular overall.

Where you install the toilet may affect the shape you choose as well. In a seldom-used powder room, the cheaper cost of a round toilet might sway you in that direction, while a bathroom that is used every day might merit the more expensive elongated version.

One last consideration for the men in the house: Functionally, elongated toilets work better for men (although they are not as usable for small children).

**COMPLEMENT CONTEMPORARY ROOM STYLES WITH A BASIC TOILET DESIGN.** A toilet does not necessarily have to be low-slung and futuristic to work well in a contemporary or even a modern bathroom. This simple two-piece toilet has an elegant and timeless look, with a modestly flared tank (along with a high-powered flush capability to prevent clogs). The flat tank top provides additional storage space akin to a small shelf, and the bright white finish works perfectly with the patterned wallpaper and plush, richly colored textiles.

**CHOOSE VINTAGE FIXTURES WITH MODERN TECHNOLOGY.** Have a hankering for vintage luxury style? Some bath fixture manufacturers cater to the restoration ideal, offering fixtures like this vintage overhead-tank toilet and bidet reproduction. The fixtures look like those of yesteryear, but the actual plumbing is updated to meet today's stricter water-use regulations and powerful flush capability. It's the best of the past and present, all in a stylish look that's hard to beat.

**ACCENT TOILETS AND BIDETS WITH HARDWARE.** The expense is relatively modest, but the boost to your bathroom's design is extravagant. This is a great place to incorporate really distinctive materials that you might not use throughout the bathroom, such as the gold fittings shown here. The fittings and other essential accessories (such as the toilet brush set) give you a chance to add vivid color, unusual materials or one-of-kind finishes without overwhelming the room's design.

**GET EUROPEAN WITH A TANKLESS TOILET.** You need to have the right type of plumbing, but where you do, you can install a tankless, pressure-assist toilet. This toilet has a distinctly European look and complements the bidet perfectly. It's also a natural partner to this bistro-style aesthetic, created with checkerboard flooring and simple wood-framed mirrors over the fixtures.

**PLEASE THE EYE WITH A UNIBODY DESIGN.** One-piece toilets (the tank is not separate from the bowl) have been around for a while now, but manufacturers continue to streamline the look while making the toilets both better at conserving water and flushing more powerfully. This clean appearance is especially effective when placed against a stunningly tiled surface, such as the marble floor and wall in this bathroom. The toilet complements the luxurious veining of the stone and allows the tile to be the star.

◀ **TURN TO TRADITION FOR COMFORT.** A traditionally styled toilet is a solid thing on which to sit, and the elongated seat of this classic model offers a great deal of comfort. Although the toilet takes up several inches more floor space than a comparable round model, that's not a worry in a large, well-designed bathroom such as this. The solid look of the toilet meshes well with the double-capacity tub and expansive double-sink vanity.

▼ **MATCH THE SIZE AND SHAPE OF THE TOILET TO THE SIZE, SHAPE, AND SCOPE OF THE BATHROOM.** This small, luxurious bathroom is compact but beautiful. But function has to be kept in mind at all times in any bathroom, and the use of a small, unibody, streamlined toilet opens up space for traffic flow and prevents the room from seeming crowded. Aesthetically, the toilet also provides a visual counterpoint to the glass sink and matte-finish tub, increasing visual interest.

# Stunning Sink Colors

**COLOR THE BATHROOM WITH A SINK.** Think twice before jumping at that pure white sink on display; there are myriad other sink color options from which to choose. Although white is the most popular and common color, off-whites and beiges work equally well in a range of bathroom designs. Faux stone surface appearances are also a great choice for a range of different room styles. Of course, you can go a bit wilder too. Most colored sinks are special-order, so allow 4 to 6 weeks.

**CHOOSE THE UNUSUAL FOR A STANDARD DROP-IN.** Don't fall into the trap of thinking a drop-in sink needs to be staid. You have many of the same options in drop-in units as you do in vessel sinks. The hammered copper sink in this vanity is just one example. The surface is fascinating to behold and equally fascinating to touch. By choosing matching faucets, the homeowner has created a nicely unified look and even helped the environment—this sink is made from recycled materials.

**COMPLEMENT THE VANITY.** The design of a drop-in sink most often takes its cue from the style set by the vanity. This hand-hammered sink offers an incredibly detailed rough-hewn finish that matches the wood vanity and antiqued faucet, as well as the brighter copper frame on the mirror. As distinctive as it might be, every bathroom sink is part of a grouping of design elements that must work together.

**UNDERMOUNT SINKS CAN BE DRAMATIC.** Moderate the power of an extremely distinctive sink by using an undermount version; the one-of-kind surface treatment is revealed only as a person approaches the vanity. This brushed nickel sink with its hammered "petal" bowl design is spectacular, perfectly matched with a brushed nickel faucet. The plain white solid-surface countertop allows the sink to dazzle close up and keeps it from overwhelming the bathroom's aesthetic from other vantage points in the room.

**CREATE VISUAL SURPRISE WITH A SINK.** When it comes to bathroom sinks, think outside the confines of the vanity countertop if you want to make a truly surprising and original design statement. This nickel sink is an undermount version of a drop-in form, but with a twist: it has a front apron that projects out of a cutout in the front edge of the counter. This is obviously a special installation, but one that never lacks for attention.

◀ **INSTALL UNDERMOUNT SINKS FOR A TRULY CONTEMPORARY OR MODERN LOOK.** The sleek, simple appearance of an undermount sink (or two, as is the case in this bathroom) is the ideal complement to a stylishly curvy, minimal, wall-mounted vanity, and achromatic tiles, like the decorative elements in this chic bathroom. This type of sink also keeps the vanity top cleaner than other styles because there is very little runover or splashing.

▼ **INJECT THE UNEXPECTED WITH AN APRON SINK.** This hybrid form, between a drop-in and an undermount, is an unusual and entirely different look for a bathroom. The style nests in an alcove in the vanity and appears visually heavy. It helps if the sink is actually a weighty material, such as the hammered copper shown here, but enameled cast iron or even a hefty porcelain unit will work just as well. You'll need to have the right type of vanity, though—it has to be thick enough to accommodate the height of the apron.

**CAPITALIZE ON THE POWER OF CONTRAST TO MAKE THE MOST OF YOUR UNDERMOUNT SINK.** Using a different material and color for the vanity type (keeping in mind that the exposed edge must be attractive) is a great way to create visual tension between an undermount sink and the surrounding surface. Here, a blank white sink is counterpoint to the pattern and color of the counter. The principle of contrast is carried through in this room's design with the installation of a sophisticated, dual-tone faucet. The faucet is a showpiece and pops against the stage of the brown counter and white sink.

◄ **ADD A BACKDROP TO WALL-MOUNT SINKS.** Make your wall-mount sink sing by using a half-height wall covering behind it. The wall surface acts almost as a canvas, emphasizing the style of the sink. However, if you use this design technique, it's best if the plumbing is concealed; this sink is formed with a trap cover as part of the sink's body. It's also a good idea to use accents that complement the sink, such as the sleek faucet, soap tray, and towel ring included here.

◄▼ **CHOOSE WALL-MOUNTS FOR DIVERSITY.** Pick a wall-mount sink for the space-saving aspects, and you can choose from among an incredible diversity of styles. Looks range from sedate contemporary styles to extreme country versions. This half-barrel wall-mounted vanity is topped with a single-surface hammered-copper counter and sink. The look isn't right for every bathroom, but in the right style of home, it makes an impressive statement.

▼ **HIDE THE PLUMBING.** Don't shy away from choosing a wall-mount sink just because you fear the plumbing will show. Manufacturers have long since answered that problem with solutions like this chrome trap cover. Wall-mount sinks can always be as sleek and hip as any other type, so if space constraints are a concern, you have an option.

**LEVERAGE BASIC SHAPES, COLORS, PATTERNS, AND FINISHES IN A BATHROOM MEANT TO HAVE A CALMING DÉCOR.** The square sink in this room is simplicity itself, and it is a perfect partner to the gray walls, elegant L-shaped faucet, an unadorned tailpiece, and some simple accents. It often doesn't take fireworks to make a show-stopping interior in the bathroom, as this one proves beyond a shadow of a doubt.

◀ **EMBELLISH A WALL-MOUNT SINK WITH ACCENTS.** Use small details to embellish the relatively simple form of most wall-mounted sinks. The curved front edge of this sink is complemented with a curving piece of metal below it, there for nothing more than a decorative flourish (and also serving as a hand-towel rack). The gooseneck faucet is a graceful accent playing off the other curving shapes.

▲ **MATCH SINK SHAPE TO OTHER FIXTURES.** Look for guidance in choosing a sink by taking cues from the room's style. Here, a modern look and rectangular bathtub are perfectly partnered with a blocky wall-mounted sink. The shape means more space in the bowl than there would be with a round sink, and the lines of the sink—as well as the modern faucet—blend perfectly with the other decorative elements.

# Stately Pedestal & Vessel Sinks

◀ **PANACHE IT UP WITH A CONSOLE SINK.** Add simple elegance to a small bathroom with a sophisticated, compact console sink. This style comes in both curving and square shapes, but both feature chrome legs with crossbars that can be used to hang towels. Add a bit of storage by buying a unit with a lower shelf. The glass shelf is a good way to incorporate a useful surface without weighing down the airy and stylish appearance a console sink brings to a room.

▼ **REDEFINE THE CONSOLE SINK TO SUIT YOUR OWN BATHROOM VISION.** This unusual model sports a unique wood frame that ties the sink structure in with frame of the mirror above and the shower mat. The spare lines and light visual weight of the console assembly is in keeping with the simple, minimal look of the space, but it also has an elegance all its own. In addition, the cross braces can be used to hang towels as needed.

**REINTERPRET STANDARD SINK STYLES.** Don't feel you have to stick to white porcelain and chrome just because you want the open and airy look of a console sink. This model is an example of a complete reinterpretation of the style. An iron base holds a hammered copper body with integral sink. It's a completely unique look, dark and dramatic. The unit includes a shelf underneath and lots of deck space for a soap dish and anything else you might want to put there. A matching faucet caps off a look that is rich in texture and wholly unexpected.

**MODERN ROOMS INVITE INNOVATION.** If modern style is your look of choice for a bathroom, consider a modern interpretation of the pedestal sink. This cylindrical sink offers a stunning design element for the right bathroom. All the plumbing is concealed. The form is alluring, and it works perfectly when combined with other modern elements, such as the floating shelves and floor-mounted faucet.

▲ **DIAL BACK SINK STYLE IN LIVELY DECOR.** A plain pedestal sink is often best for a bathroom featuring other exceptionally dynamic elements. The reflective red walls in this room dominate the space and grab the attention. Unembellished features, including a simple toilet and uncomplicated pedestal sink, allow the surface treatment to shine while still providing handsome visual features.

◀▲ **FLOWING FORMS MAKE PEDESTALS STAND OUT.** Add a bit of flair to a contemporary bathroom with a curvy, sensuous pedestal shape. Pedestal sinks can be plain or ornate, but a shape such as this makes a vivid first impression and works perfectly with a detailed tile pattern, such as the black wall surface behind this sink. The sleek single-handled faucet is also well matched to the sink.

◀ **CHOOSE STYLISH PEDESTALS FOR INCREASED APPEAL.** Even pedestal sinks can have design flair. This period-style sink brings a flourish to this stunning bathroom, popping out against a background of cobalt tiles and sitting between a toilet and bidet styled for the same time period. Both the pedestal and bowl are highly designed and detailed, creating a visual appeal far beyond the simple form or function of the fixture.

▶ **CREATE A FOCAL POINT WITH UNUSUAL MATERIALS.** Looking for a standout sink? Vessel sinks may be the perfect option for you, and they are available in an astounding selection of materials and forms. This example is one of the more unusual, crafted in a slightly irregular oval of green onyx with the appearance inside of an abalone shell. It's a distinctive style that works perfectly with the surrounding decorative elements.

▽ **METAL VESSELS CAN MAKE A DESIGN.** Metal vessel sinks are becoming increasingly popular, and if you want to add unique textures and interesting finishes to your bathroom, you could do a lot worse than one of these incredibly interesting fixtures. This formed metal bowl carries a tempered copper finish, with distinct mottling that makes it different from any other sink. A material such as this is best matched to other raw materials in the room, such as the interwoven copper wall surface and stone vanity counter.

**SIMPLE VESSEL SINKS ARE ALWAYS IN STYLE.** Add a modern look to a shared bathroom with simple and square his-and-her sinks mounted on top of a wall-hung slab. Where the plumbing runs behind the vessel, such as with these generous sinks, the drain can be run through the slab so that it's not visible from the top. This discreet placement creates a sleek appearance made even sleeker with the addition of a stainless steel rod on the front of the slab—the perfect hand-towel rack. Although you'll sacrifice some storage with a design like this, the open area under the sink increases the sense of space in the room.

**CHOOSE A NICKEL FINISH FOR A SOPHISTICATED LOOK.** Put a contemporary spin on a metal vessel sink by choosing one with a nickel finish. The finish is different enough from chrome to set itself apart, and this hand-worked metal vessel brings textural variations that highlight the beautiful finish. Take the easy road and match a nickel-finish sink to a brushed-nickel faucet and handles, as seen in this bathroom.

**MOUNT VESSELS WITH WIT.** Use a vessel sink to craft a one-of-kind look full of personality. This box-shaped stone vessel sink has been mounted offset from blocks framed out from the wall and clad in different types of stone. Coupled with a long, skinny mirror, orb lighting, and a wall-mount faucet, the look is full of style and surprise. You can create an equally impressive scene by placing your vessel sink in an unusual relationship to the counter or support.

**MOUNT GLASS ON GLASS.** If vessel sinks have captured your imagination, you'll find clear glass vessel sinks almost magical in how they confuse the eye. Water in the sink seems to almost be floating in midair, and the illusion is made even stronger by mounting the sink on a glass vanity counter. The look isn't right for every bathroom, but it can be stunning in a modern or streamlined contemporary bathroom—especially when coupled with a support such as this dark wood pillar. A combination like this can even serve as the focal point of a powder room.

**DOUBLE UP WITH A TRAY SINK.** Sometimes called "trough" sinks, these are uncommon but unique, and perfect for double-faucet bathrooms used by more than one person at a time. The sink is often used in place of his-and-her sinks, and this particular version is made of painted volcanic rock, with a back-edge drain. A vessel sink such as this can be a design centerpiece in the bathroom. Just be careful in choosing colorful sinks, because overly bold or trendy colors can become dated rather quickly.

**SURPRISE AND DELIGHT THE EYE WITH A NEARLY FLAT VESSEL SINK.** When super-stylish elegance is your bathroom design goal, consider a "plate" vessel sink. These sinks are almost flat and defy the traditional description of a sink, but work just as well as any other. However, you do need to be a little careful when matching a faucet to such a shallow sink, to avoid splashing (adjusting water pressure can also control this). For an even more impressive effect, turn to a material such as nickel-finish hammered metal, used here.

▲ **USE SQUARE SINKS FOR ROOMY BASINS.** Choose a square vessel when you want a lot of room in the bowl of the sink and where the shape complements other linear elements in the room design. The large white porcelain sink in this room goes perfectly with the shape of the vanity structure.

▲▶ **WEDGE VESSEL SINKS IN CORNERS.** Vessel sinks are great solutions in tight spots because of their open appeal. This bathroom features a hammered copper sink with a rough natural texture that works well with the stone surfaces and faux wood timber counter support in the space. The effect created is a natural look, warm, comfortable and informal. The sink is just one standout element among many.

▶ **STONE VESSEL SINKS IMPRESS.** Consider a stone vessel sink to make a big impression in a smaller space such as a powder room. Material such as unpolished marble contributes a rich texture and feel to the room. Stone sinks are a little pricier than other types, and they may need to be sealed against water and stain infiltration, but the end result is spectacular.

▶ **CONTEMPORARY CALLS FOR STREAMLINED SINKS.** Stretch the definition of a vessel sink by using a countertop "tray" version such as this stone sink. This streamlined look is right at home in a contemporary bathroom. The basin is gently sloped for an unusual geometric appearance; the vanity counter is sized to perfectly complement the sink. It's a pleasing appearance that is easy to re-create regardless of the type of square or rectangular vessel sink you choose.

▼ **PLAY WITH VESSEL MOUNTING STYLE.** Achieve interesting effects by using vessel sinks in unusual ways. Here, a clear glass vessel sink has been embedded in a floating glass countertop anchored to the wall by way of a wood frame. The chrome plumbing, fixtures, and accents contribute to a clean, modern aesthetic, but the sink's relationship to the countertop is really the key visual in this area of the bathroom.

▲ **CREATE A CLASSIC LOOK WITH VITREOUS CHINA.** This material makes for an incredibly elegant and delicate vessel sink. The high-gloss finish and the fact that china sinks can be manufactured with relief patterns, such as the floral motif shown here, make this option extremely attractive to homeowners looking for that little something extra in their bathroom design. However, these types of sinks are most at home in more formal or traditional bathrooms.

◄ **PARTNER YOUR LINEAR VESSEL SINK WITH A LINEAR FAUCET.** This is a natural marriage, especially because the other fixtures and decorative elements in a bathroom are so often linear in nature—from tile, to mirrors, to towel bars. Carrying through a shape such as lines, squares, and blocks can be a way to help the eye make sense of the room's entire design. Repetition of shape elements is usually a safe, reliable, and pleasing factor in bathrooms and other rooms alike. And it doesn't hurt when you use upscale elements like this finely made sink and super stylish faucet.

▼ **MATCH A VISUALLY STRIKING FAUCET TO A SHOWCASE VESSEL SINK.** The impressive visual of a one-of-a-kind vessel sink calls for a faucet design that will not be overpowered by the sink. Here, a hammered metal sink is a focal point in the room, but it is wisely paired with a modern wall mount faucet that also grabs the eye. Notice that the faucet is a shiny chrome in contrast to the matte surface of the sink—a great way to add some visual tension.

**EXPLOIT SUBTLETY WHEN IT'S SOPHISTICATED SUBTLETY.**
Although the color of this sink is a little unusual, it might
not jump out at you. But upon close inspection, the color
is nearly luminous, deep and rich with a satin finish. That's
because the color is enamel applied over volcanic rock, which
takes the coating in a specific and unique way. It also means
the sink is super durable. Although the company produces
fixtures in every color of the rainbow, this color perfectly
complements the wall tiles and the dark wood of the vanity.
Easy to clean, sensuously curved, and just the right size, this
sink is perfect for the room.

# EXCEPTIONAL HARDWARE

Divine Faucets

Superior Showerheads

Fantastic Tub Faucets

As the designs of sinks and bathtubs proliferate and shower enclosures grow ever more stylish and sophisticated, it should come as no surprise that the fixtures that service those areas are evolving as well. The forms, finishes, and positioning of faucets, showerheads, and controls are all increasing right along with the other fixtures in the modern bathroom.

Touch faucets—those that operate without the need for a handle—are not as popular as they once were because so many user-friendly handle types have hit the market. These faucets merge undeniable style with controls that are easy for children and anyone with functional impairments to use. The manufacturers simply took ease of use as a design challenge and ran with

it. More and more, every faucet is super easy to use and functions flawlessly.

New showerhead design is also about adaptability and flexibility. The focus is on a multihead experience not only for those who can afford a custom-built enclosure, but for everyone. This usually translates to a fixed head, partnered with a mounted handheld showerhead that can be positioned along a bar or held. The latest showerhead technology includes Bluetooth speakers and LED lights, but the emphasis remains on the basic function of the showerhead—making for an enjoyable daily shower. Fortunately, with all the possibilities among faucets and showerheads, you'll never have to surrender function to form.

**GO GOOSENECK TO ADD ELEGANCE TO THE SINK.** Gooseneck faucets are some of the most popular because their graceful form embellishes the appearance of any sink. If you want an even more upscale appearance, choose a gold-toned finish like the one on this faucet. The look is very chic and contrasts vividly with the machined surfaces of the faucet to make this sink fixture a true attention-grabber.

**A SPECIAL SINK CALLS FOR A SPECIAL FAUCET.**
This concrete sink with edge drain is an over-the-top feature begging for a faucet as equally stunning. This three-hole modern version mightily answers the call. The crude, rough texture of the stone contrasts the super-smooth polished nickel surface of the faucet, and the faucet's clean, curving lines pop out against the rough, hard lines of the sink. It's a marriage of contrast, but one that works beautifully.

▲ **MOUNT UNUSUAL FAUCETS ON SIMPLE SINKS.**
The accents you choose in a small bathroom
have a lot of visual power. Even a small detail
such as a faucet can affect the look of the
room—especially a distinctive faucet such as
this. The porcelain body forms a pitcher for
the water, while the metal handle controls the
flow. It's a wonderful combination and a truly
interesting visual that livens up the bathroom.

◀ ▲ **PAIR DARK FAUCETS WITH DARK
FURNISHINGS.** Antiqued faucet finishes continue
to be popular, and it's a style that might work
well in your bathroom—especially if your
bathroom furniture is finished dark brown or
ebony. This bathroom's taupe walls complement
the color of the faucet, and accessories match
to create a lovely unified design. Crisp white
wainscoting ensures that the antiqued finishes
and darker colors don't overwhelm the space.

◀ **DO JUSTICE TO DISTINCTIVE DECORS WITH
EXTREME FAUCET DESIGNS.** Choose a highly
evocative faucet to match your particular
aesthetic when you're designing a bathroom in
a distinctive style. This modern bathroom called
for accents that reinforced the angular, linear
nature of the room. The faucet—and the light
fixture that complements it—plays right into
the design style while being almost a work of
art itself. Enlightened selection of accents such
as faucets can make or break a bathroom's look
and feel.

**PICK A WALL-MOUNT FAUCET TO SUIT ROOM STYLE.** Most wall-mounted faucets are crafted in a contemporary or modern style, but that's not a hard-and-fast rule. When you need a wall-mounted faucet for a more distinct style of sink, such as the antiqued hand-wrought finish of this undermount, or when your choice of vanity top has no holes, you can find one to match. This country-style faucet is a perfect example.

**ADD WHIMSY WITH A WATERFALL FAUCET.** Looking for something different in your contemporary bathroom? Look no further. A waterfall faucet looks whimsical when it's running and sleek when it's not. This stunning accent can be a big part of the room's design, but won't break the bank. Just make sure that you don't fall in love with the faucet to the exclusion of the sink! This is a distinctive, contemporary style that isn't right for every sink or every bathroom. It calls for a simpler, linear sink to show it at its best.

**USE CLASSIC FAUCETS WITH CLASSIC DECORATIVE ELEMENTS.** The wisest move is often to match your faucet choice to your bathroom style. Although many wild faucet designs are made and sold, classic is best for a room like this, which features traditional wainscoting and a traditionally styled pedestal sink. The chrome finish complements the sink, and the elegant gooseneck form is ideal for this setting.

◄ **CAREFULLY MATCH YOUR FAUCET TO YOUR SINK FOR A VISUAL THAT IS MUCH MORE THAN THE SUM OF ITS PARTS.** Choosing the perfect faucet for any sink is both art and science, but take cues from the sink's shape and you'll rarely go wrong. The elegant L faucet coupled with this vessel sink contains the same circular aspect in its tubular form as the sink does in its overall shape. The chrome finish goes perfectly with the white porcelain sink—a natural, classic marriage that you can replicate in your own bathroom.

◄ ▼ **INTRODUCE AN EASIER-TO-CLEAN FAUCET SURFACE BY CHOOSING BRUSHED NICKEL FINISHES.** Chrome may still be king when it comes to bathroom faucets, but chrome shows fingerprints, water spots, and more. That means near-constant cleaning. If you want to make life a little easier for yourself, select a faucet with a sophisticated brushed-nickel finish, such as the one shown here. As this faucet proves, the finish is just as elegant as chrome and melds with all the vanity top materials that a chrome faucet complements.

▼ **BLACK IS THE NEW BLACK.** Matte black finishes are finding a place in bathrooms of all design styles because of the pure, unadulterated drama the look brings. It's a matter of contrast; there are rarely matte black surfaces in a bathroom. Coloring relatively small design features this way allows you to introduce the look without overwhelming the room. Black is also a wonderful partner to white porcelain, the marble surface shown here, and most other surfaces found in bathrooms. The finish integrates surprisingly well into a space more commonly associated with white, and including a matte black faucet is a way to experiment with the look in your bathroom without risking much.

**OPT FOR EASY-TO-USE LEVER HANDLES.** This type of handle is easiest for young children, the elderly, or people with disabilities. Levers require far less grip strength than conventional twist handles, and they look fantastic. The styling of lever handles can be elegantly lyrical and is sometimes just as stunning as the design of the faucet body. Just be sure that the lever handles you choose will clear the lip of any top-mount or vessel sink.

**SQUARE AWAY YOUR FAUCET TO MATCH THE SPACE.** Bathroom faucet spouts are most commonly tubular, but they don't have to be. Where the room is all lines, angles, and blocky shapes, it makes a lot of sense to pick a squared-off spout. The water flows the same, but the look is totally eye-catching. Notice how the handles on this modern faucet are in keeping with the generally linear theme. The clean chrome finish reinforces the simplicity of the design, and the design itself fits right in with the hard lines of the subway tile, mirror, and sink basin. However, this type of faucet could also be quite effective used to contrast a rounded sink.

▶ **MAKE THE MOST OF NEW MODERN FAUCETS BY SHOWING THEM OFF IN A SLEEK BATHROOM.** Solid-surface sinks are the ideal partner for futuristic faucets such as these, allowing the stunning shapes to really pop and become focal points in the room. The choice of single-handle faucets is in keeping with the clean, streamlined aesthetic of this room, and the finish matches the sheen of the tiles on the backsplash and the surfaces of the vanity and countertop.

▼ **CONSIDER HOW THE FAUCET WILL PLAY AGAINST THE WALL SURFACE.** Chrome fixtures and accents might have worked in this bathroom, but a brushed-nickel widespread faucet and matching towel ring are simply stunning against a wall painted dark charcoal with a satin finish. Because of the light, similar shade of the whitewashed wood vanity, the faucet would have faded into the background of a white or cream wall. Always keep in mind that even something as small as a faucet is part of a unified visual impression in the confines of a bathroom.

**▲ GO BOLD WITH A WALL-MOUNT FAUCET.** If you've gone to the trouble of plumbing a wall-mounted faucet, it makes no sense to install a wallflower version that won't grab attention. The model here not only has an attractive curving shape and easy-to-use handles, its black finish stands in stark contrast to the marble vanity top and textured white backsplash. Notice that even the finish, a simple matte, contrasts the surfaces around the faucet.

**▶ CHANNEL YOUR INNER DESIGNER WITH A DARING REINTERPRETATION OF THE BASIC FAUCET SPOUT.** Echoing the design of a Roman aqueduct, this faucet—and those like it—play with the concept of what form a bathroom faucet spout should take. It's a witty spin on something that is so accepted and part of the bathroom landscape that it has an outsize impact on the impression of the room. Choosing a faucet such as this one can be a simple, beautiful way to upend conventional notions in the room.

▲ **HELP YOUR FAUCET POP.** Sometimes, a faucet should simple accent the vanity top or sink with which it's paired. But where the room is ripe with luxury elements, such as the high-end tile, chic over-sink light fixture and unique console sink in this room, the faucet needs to announce itself. A two-tone, black-body, classically styled model is ideal. The faucet contrasts the elements around it, but not in a jarring way.

KALLISTA

▲ TAKE A PAGE FROM TIFFANY'S BOOK WHEN
CHOOSING A LUXURY FAUCET FOR YOUR DECADENT
MASTER BATH. The number of alluring finishes
available on bathroom faucets continues to
multiply, but one of the most chic you can
choose is this silver finish that makes the faucet
look like fine jewelry dropped onto the lip of the
countertop. Inlaid Mother-of-Pearl handles set
off a poetic shape ripe with timeless style. The
faucet is perfectly paired with a marble vanity
top—a finish like this always calls out for pairing
with other luxury surfaces. The simple white
undermount sink provides a wonderful, clean
backdrop to the showcase faucet.

▶ DON'T FORGET THE HANDLES WHEN SHOPPING
FOR A WIDESPREAD FAUCET. Increasingly,
manufacturers are offering high-end options
for the handles in addition to luxury finishes
on their faucets. The handles can be crystal
or glass such as the ones shown here, or hand
painted, inlaid, or otherwise made special in
their own right. However, in any case, make
sure the handles are usable in your home; the
spin handles shown here might not be the best
choice for a universal design bathroom.

◄ **SPICE UP A LOW-KEY BATHROOM WITH A SPACE-AGE SHAPE.** This simple L faucet looks like it's about to take flight, thanks to flared bases on both the spout and the handles. It's a simple look, but also arresting, fun, and timeless. Unusual shapes are a great way to break up what is all too often a tyranny of straight lines in the bathroom.

▼ **ENSURE EASE OF OPERATION FOR ANY WALL-MOUNTED FAUCET.** This stunning gold fixture absolutely pops out of the detailed tile background and adds an undeniably upscale look to the sink. But any wall-mount faucet has to take practicality into account. Here, the equivalent of paddle handles guarantees that the faucet will be as easy to operate as it is on the eyes. Smooth operation and fabulous good looks are an ideal combination to shoot for in your bathroom faucet shopping adventures.

**THE FIXTURES MAKE THE SHOWER.** Add special shower fixtures to turn even a modest shower stall into a luxurious enclosure. Fixtures such as the body-side spray nozzles lining the tiled walls of this shower create a full-body shower experience. This shower also includes a stunning rainwater showerhead and a handheld showerhead connected to an adjustable bar. All the different spray points make it possible to adjust the shower for any particular desired strength, direction, or combination of sprays.

▲ **ADD DISTINCTIVE LUXURY AND STYLE WITH UNCONVENTIONAL SHOWER FIXTURES.** Don't be trapped by tradition when it comes to selecting showerheads and spray fixtures. Although wall nozzles and overhead "rain" showerheads are more common, institute a unique appearance by choosing wall spray tiles and a blocky showerhead. These fixtures, including the head, are adjustable and can be set to different types of spray pattern. The look is slick, chic, and extraordinary—just right for a distinctive shower with slate-tiled walls and wood accents.

▶▲ **ENJOY MULTIHEAD LUXURY WITH THE SIMPLE INSTALLATION OF A SINGLE SHOWERHEAD.** Manufacturers have responded to consumers' enthusiasm for multiple showerheads in a number of innovative ways. This showerhead is one example, and it is actually two adjustable showerheads in one. It provides invigorating cross sprays in a head that can be installed in minutes, and the fixture itself is elegant and eye-catching, gleaming with a polished nickel finish.

▶ **USE SQUARE FIXTURES WHERE ROUND IS EXPECTED.** Introduce a cool accent to a contemporary shower enclosure by using a showerhead and hardware in unexpected shapes. The "cube" fixtures here are visually interesting and surprising, reinterpreting the traditional round shape of a showerhead and controls. The shape of these elements complements the shape of the shower enclosure itself, as well as the frameless glass wall.

▲ **TOWERS ENRICH SHOWERS.** Complete shower consoles (also known as "towers") are impressive additions to even a modest shower enclosure. The look is sleek and modern and well suited to a chic surface, such as this surround covered in mosaic glass tiles. The console routes water to the showerhead and serves as the central control tower for the shower, including an array of spray heads that can be opened or closed to suit the individual. It's a luxurious shower experience no matter how you look at it.

▲ ▶ **USE SIMPLE SHOWERHEADS ON SIMPLE SURFACES.** Despite the temptingly sophisticated and complex showerhead systems with additional features like steam heads, it is often the case that a simple solution works as well or better. This basic, single-handle showerhead looks just right against a backdrop of old-world stone tile. It was also easy to install because the plumbing from the handle to the head is piped outside the wall, rather than being plumbed inside it. The large showerhead still provides a refreshing shower experience and looks great while doing so.

▶ **LUXURIATE WITH MULTIPLE SHOWERHEADS.** Several showerheads spraying in multiple directions provide one of the most invigorating showers you'll ever experience. The key is adjustability. The shower sprayers on the side wall in this enclosure can be turned off, as can the hand sprayer. You can completely control how much or little spray the shower provides. Notice the antique styling of the heads in this shower; they blend perfectly with the mottled wall surfacing.

▲ **MAKE SHOWERING AS HANDY AS POSSIBLE WITH AN ADJUSTABLE BAR AND HANDHELD SHOWERHEAD.** Slide-bar showerheads are some of the most useful models, because the spray can be adjusted to any height along the bar. Most slide-bar sets come equipped with a handheld showerhead that is secured in a bracket when not in your hand. As useful as it is, there's no denying that the bar adds an attractive vertical element within the shower enclosure.

◄ **COLOR YOUR SHOWER TO SUIT YOUR MOOD.** Showerheads that incorporate colored LED lights are a recent innovation that allows you to adjust the mood in your shower to suit your own preference. The changeable colors also create drama in an otherwise sedate space. You'll find LED-colored lights in other fixtures as well, from bathtub lights to mirror backlighting. You can even coordinate the lighting across the fixtures in the room.

# Fantastic Tub Faucets

▲ **EXPLOIT THE DESIGN POTENTIAL OF TUB FAUCETS.** It's easy to overlook the hardware when you become enamored of a stylish freestanding tub, but that would be a mistake. As this example shows, tub faucets can be poetic in their elegance. This faucet features a classic gooseneck spout and a separate handheld spray head for washing the shampoo out of your hair. As useful as it is, this is just as much a design accent that improves the look of the room.

▶ ▲ **ENSURE SUCCESS BY MATCHING THE FAUCET FINISH TO THE TUB.** If your tub has a unique finish, such as the brushed nickel of this pedestal tub, you can play it safe by using a faucet in a matching finish, allowing the tub's appearance to take center stage. This faucet doesn't give up any style points with its elegant gooseneck spout and hand-held wand attachment. It's an ideal pairing between hardware and tub.

▶ **COMBINE ELEGANCE AND EASE WITH HIGH-END FIXTURES FOR A WALK-IN TUB.** Just because a walk-in tub is made for accessibility doesn't mean it shouldn't be stylish. These simple tub fixtures show how basic elegance and a classic chrome finish can add lovely clean elements to the otherwise fairly plain tub. The controls and the spray head are designed to be easy to use and hold, and the gooseneck faucet simply takes its shape from those cues.

▲ **EMBELLISH DISTINCTIVE TUBS WITH STYLED FAUCETS.**
A country-style deck-mounted tub is well served by an
impressive faucet with a telephone-style cradle for the
handheld sprayer attachment. A clean, chrome finish is a
natural choice for a homey, white room such as this, and the
ornate style of the faucet really shines against the plainer
background of white wainscoting and matching tub surround.
The faucet is also perfectly placed to be handy for anyone
taking a bath.

◄▲ **SIMPLE TUB FAUCETS FIT MOST TUB STYLES.** Turn to
modern and minimal faucet styles for a floor-mount faucet
that suits many different bathroom and bathtub styles. This
casual and informal bathroom includes a tub with an old-time
rolled lip and hanging kettle bells, but the elegant and spare
gooseneck faucet—supported on a small circular foot—blends
right in without making much noise. It's a lovely accent that
doesn't overpower or confuse the look of the room.

◄ **PLAY WITH BATHTUB FAUCET PLACEMENT.** Don't be a slave
to convention when choosing where to place your bathtub
faucet. Depending on the type of tub you have and where
it's located in the bathroom, there may be several different
potential locations for the faucet. Positioning such as this,
with the faucet on one side and the controls on the other,
creates a balanced and interesting look. It also moves the
faucet away from the ends of the tub, where a bather's head
is most likely to rest.

# THE WELL-LIT BATHROOM

Marvelous Vanity Lights

Ideal General Fixtures

The right lighting is crucial for keeping a bathroom safe and putting the best face on the room's design. The best bathroom lighting accommodates different users and many different situations. It must ensure against trips or falls as bathers get in and out of a tub and make any face in the vanity mirror look as close to what will be seen in daylight as possible. The fixtures themselves should look good or at least be subtle enough not to affect the design in a negative way.

Achieving all those goals usually requires different types of lighting throughout a bathroom. A general ambient light source is essential for any bathroom, from a powder room to a large,

luxurious master bathroom. Most bathrooms will also need the proper mirror lighting, as well as specific lighting for areas such as a standalone shower enclosure.

Various types of lighting combine to show off your decorative elements without annoying shadows or hot spots. Certain fixtures can also become decorative elements, especially those used around the mirror. You can find fixtures in any type of style, from country farmhouse to modern. Whichever you choose, always make sure the illumination they supply is all the light the room needs to shine.

**BALANCE VANITY LIGHTING TO PUT YOUR BEST FACE FORWARD.** Long vanities with undivided mirrors on the wall require creative lighting to make the image in the mirror as true to life as possible. Here, strong side lights are used to project light across the mirror, but highlights positioned over the vanity offer fill lighting. When coordinating two or more sets of lights like this, put the lights on a dimmer switch whenever possible. That will let you adjust the lighting to the level of illumination that works best for you.

◄ **CONTROL BATHROOM LIGHTING.** Put strong vanity lights—and all lights in the bathroom, if you can—on a dimmer switch. The bright lights on either side of this framed vanity mirror leave the image in the mirror crystal clear, but they sometimes may be too bright for users' comfort. In those instances, dim the lights to create a lovely mood or simply to suit an individual's preference.

◄▼ **LIGHT DUAL MIRRORS EVENLY.** The most common placement for vanity lights is on either side of the mirror. This particular bathroom matches his-and-her mirrors to the twin sinks below, creating a very symmetrical look. The best way to light dual mirrors is to use three fixtures so that each mirror is lit from both sides. These fixtures are fitted with elegant shades that look lovely but, more importantly, prevent any hot spots in the field of view and create a nice, diffused light.

▼ **MINIMIZE LIGHT REFLECTION WITH MUTED TOP LIGHTS.** Where it's impractical to install lights along the sides of a vanity mirror, you still need to use lights specifically for the mirror area. Many times, this involves adding a strip of lights over the top of the mirror. These lights were carefully positioned high enough so there are no bright spot reflections for anyone looking in the mirror. The plastic shades diffuse the light, which helps avoid dark facial shadows that occur when strong light is directed down the mirror.

▲ **LIGHT FOR SAFETY.** A single overhead light such as this can work perfectly for ensuring safety around a tub or shower. The light can be put on a separate switch or added to an existing circuit. The light may not seem overpowering, but it only needs to give the eye a clear idea of where water has splashed and where the floor and tub deck are dry.

▶ ▲ **USE RECESSED CEILING LIGHTS WHEREVER YOU NEED BRIGHT, CLEAR, GENERAL LIGHT.** The recessed fixtures broadcast light evenly down from the ceiling and offer an understated look suitable for many different styles of bathroom. Although they take some work to install, they can be added almost anywhere you need bright light for safety or personal grooming. The best recessed fixtures include adjustable heads, allowing you to change the direction of the light and customize the room's lighting to suit your needs or mood.

▶ **LIGHT-AND-FAN COMBOS ARE DOUBLY USEFUL.** A general overhead light fixture can serve a smaller bathroom all by itself and provide much of the light needed in a larger space. This fixture is unique in that it incorporates a vent fan into the base. Combination fan-light fixtures are useful in any bathroom that has ductwork in place for the vent.

**PICK LIGHT SHADES FOR GOOD SKIN TONES.** When using over-mirror lights such as these three fixtures, it's wise to outfit them with low-wattage, soft white bulbs. The softer light, especially diffused through a skin-flattering yellow lampshade, shows skin tones more accurately and with fewer harsh shadows. Bright is good for close personal grooming, but a softer, milder light works really well for checking your image as others see it.

**TUBE LIGHTS SERVE MOST BATHROOMS WELL.** You can use over-mirror tube lights for dispersed illumination, easy installation, and a simple, streamlined look. The appearance of the fixture fits especially well in a contemporary bathroom such as this one. If you decide to choose this type of vanity light, it's wise to use one that runs the entire width of the mirror for maximum light spread.

**RECESSED LIGHTS WORK EVERYWHERE.** Recessed ceiling lights are effective general lighting solutions, especially for an area such as the open shower shown here. Not only do the lights ensure safety in the shower and adjacent areas, but the bright halogen lights also make the stunning glass-tiled surfaces of this shower sparkle. Dress up any shower enclosure by completely tiling all the surfaces. Keep in mind that any lighting fixture used in a shower enclosure needs to be sealed against the moisture and rated for wet areas.

**DIRECT LIGHTING WITH TRACK HEADS.** Use track lighting as an adjustable source of ambient light in a large bathroom. You can purchase subtle tracks and lighting heads that blend into the design and use them where direct lighting is needed most (here, they not only create a safer environment around the tub, they also fill in the shadows left by the sconce uplights on either side of the mirror). Track lights are especially effective in a room such as this, where abundant reflective surfaces bounce and amplify the light, ensuring excellent full-room illumination.

# BATHROOM EXTRAS

Attractive Universal Design

Handy Makeup Areas

Super Saunas

Shower Accessories

Stunning Skylights & Windows

Towel Warmers

Mirror Style

Exceptional Accents

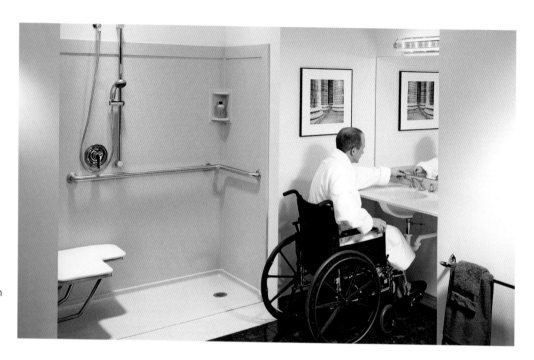

**STYLIZE SPECIAL-NEEDS FEATURES.**
Don't give up on good design simply because you have to set up the room for users with special needs. This neat, trim, and spare roll-in shower is an example of Universal Design integrated in a visually pleasing minimalist aesthetic. The sink is also adapted to suit a wheelchair user but still looks handsome enough for any bathroom. As an added bonus, both features make the bathroom easier to use whether you have special needs or not.

There are really two types of "extras" in this chapter: bit players such as the walk-on extras in a film, and other features that may or may not be required in your bathroom, but could transform the purpose and focus of the room.

The first group includes handy additions that are the icing on your bathroom design cake. They add some zest to the look of the room and can make the space a more efficient and comfortable place to spend time. Something such as a sleek European-style towel warmer falls into this category.

Other features have much more impact. Although it's certainly nice to have a towel hook, the right grab bar in the right place can save a hip-fracturing fall. That's why we've put universal design features (which encompass aging in place extras for elderly homeowners) right up front in this chapter. The great thing about these particular features is even though they are meant for use by people with physical impediments of one sort or another, they are becoming much more significant design elements within the room. That's because just a few years ago, walk-in tubs and wheelchair-accessible shower enclosures were, if not ugly, not necessarily attractive either. Now, homeowners who may not even be staring down the barrel of old age or infirmity might want to consider adding a sleek walk-in tub as a soaking feature in a smaller bathroom.

Although there are a great number of options in the pages that follow, this chapter should be considered an à la carte menu. Pick and choose the features that make the most sense for your bathroom and for the way you and your family use the space. The trick is to add only those features that will have the most impact on the look and usability of the room.

▲ **DON'T SACRIFICE STYLE FOR SUBSTANCE WHEN IT COMES TO WALK-IN TUBS.** Today's walk-in tubs are more than an accessibility feature; they can be handsome additions to the bathroom, features that conserve space and offer a luxury bathing experience. This tub includes a secure and easy-to-use door, a tub light that can be changed to different colors, and jets for a relaxing tub experience. You don't need to have a mobility issues to install or enjoy a tub such as this—a penchant for luxury and easy bathing are all that are required.

◄ **BLEND SAFETY FEATURES INTO THE DESIGN.** The Universal Design elements in this bathroom are so well integrated into the look that they hardly seem like something extra at all. Grab bars for the shower, bath, and toilet are all positioned according to established guidelines, but the brushed nickel finish really blends these features. The finish is easy on the eyes and matches the faucet and toilet paper holder. There's no reason that the accessibility features you add to your bathroom can't look this good.

**AID BATHROOM ACCESSIBILITY WITH BEAUTIFUL ERGONOMIC FIXTURES.** Add specially designed fixtures in a bathroom used by people with disabilities or coordination and mobility issues. This ergonomic showerhead is mounted on a grab bar and has special grips built in to ensure that someone with poor hand strength or other problems can hold it securely.

**NEVER FORGET THAT GRAB BARS ARE DESIGN ACCENTS.** Make your universal design bathroom as attractive as possible by blending accessibility elements into the design at large. A common, high-quality tiled wall makes this roll-in shower stall look absolutely natural, like an intentional part of the room's décor. Chrome grab bars positioned strategically throughout the room complement the chrome on the roll-under sink, which is itself elegantly styled to look like a design high point. Every element of the room's design exhibits a thoughtfulness and aesthetic savvy that improves use while improving the look of the space.

**POSITION GRAB BARS FOR MAXIMUM EFFICIENCY.** Designing a bathroom that adheres to the standards of universal design means adding specific specialized features in just the right places. Don't assume that you can use any grab bar for any application; this special crooked bar is specifically meant as an aid to use a toilet, and its position on the wall is well thought out to provide all the leverage a person with limited mobility needs to get up and down.

▲ **EXPECT A CLEAN, DETAILED LOOK FROM TODAY'S WALK-IN TUBS.** Unlike yesterday's models, modern walk-in tubs usually come equipped with full-function and attractive fixtures, such as the chrome faucet, handles, and spray head shown here. This model also features jets, which are increasingly being included in walk-in tubs. The jetted bathing experience means these tubs have become as much luxury items as they are universal design fixtures.

▶ **CONTROL YOUR BATHING EXPERIENCE.** Among the features on modern walk-in tubs, electronic controls serve two purposes. Not only do they allow bathers with hand-strength and coordination issues to easily operate the controls for the tub, but they also simplify tub operation for anyone else. But as a bonus, electronic controls such as these are also streamlined and attractive.

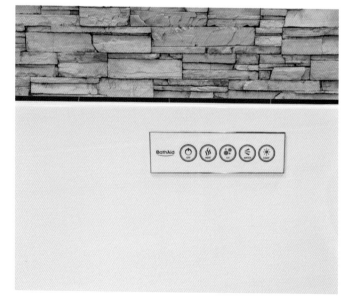

▲ **RETROFIT FOR SAFETY AND ACCESSIBILITY.** Curbed shower enclosures can be barriers to someone who must use a walker or a wheelchair. But simple rubber ramps are a quick and easy solution—and an alternative to a complete enclosure overhaul. Mats such as the ones shown here drain off excess water, have a nonslip surface, are easy to clean, and can be put in place in seconds.

◄ ▲ **BUY AN ACCESSIBLE SHOWER AS A SUITE WITH ENCLOSURE.** Want to make installing a universal design shower enclosure—complete with easy-to-use fixtures and grab bars—a breeze? Make the process smooth by purchasing one of the many complete enclosure packages available on the market. An enclosure such as the one shown here includes a ramp lip for easy wheelchair access, integral grab bars (often offered in different materials and finishes), and stunning fixtures such as the two showerheads shown here, with lever controls that are ADA compliant.

◄ **SIT PRETTY IN A UNIVERSAL DESIGN SHOWER ENCLOSURE.** It's important to consider seating in any completely accessible shower enclosure. Custom-made enclosures often have a bench built into the structure itself, but if you have a simpler enclosure, or an entirely prefab unit, chances are that seating wasn't a part of the package. No problem. You can retrofit any shower with stable, secure seating as needed. Stools and small benches such as this one, with handsome teak seat slats, are widely available. Notice the rubberized feet; the best seats have features that prevent slipping and help stabilize the seat as the bather moves around.

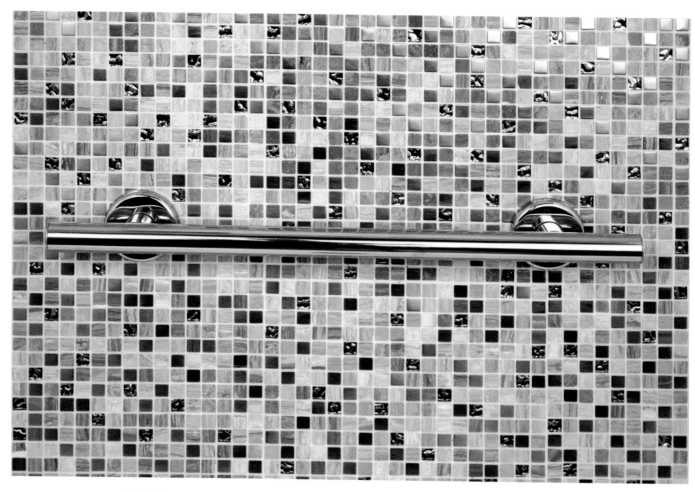

**STYLIZE ANY WALL WITH A SLEEK CHROME GRAB BAR.** Although the first generation of home bathroom grab bars were usually finished in brushed nickel because it didn't show fingerprints, chrome grab bars have become much more popular. They may require a little bit more cleaning to remain bright and shiny, but they are far more likely to complement existing fixtures in the bathroom, from faucets to towel bars. Set against mosaic tiles or other busy patterns, a chrome grab bar can really pop and become a cool design feature.

**GO WILD WITH YOUR CHOICE OF GRAB BARS.** The three examples shown here are just the tip of the iceberg of new grab bar materials and styles. Manufacturers are increasingly producing grab bars that not only do justice to your existing bathroom design, but they can actually set the tone for new room looks. Neon colors, dark or light finishes, natural or synthetic materials are all available, and all remain essential safety features.

**MAKEUP FITS IN MODEST SPACES.** You don't necessarily need a lot of room for a well-appointed makeup area. This wonderful small desk addition to the side of a detailed vanity provides all the space necessary for the lady of the house to paint her nails or apply lipstick and makeup. The cushioned upholstered chair is a great addition and an ideal element in any makeup area.

**BUY A SAUNA KIT FOR YOUR CORNER.**
Do you have a lot of extra room in your bathroom and want to add a big luxury feature? A sauna is a healthy retreat from the day's stress and comfortably fits in the corner of a larger bathroom. Saunas such as this are often sold as complete kits—just be sure you measure carefully to ensure the finished structure fits properly into the available space.

**CORNER SAUNAS FIT TIGHT SPOTS.**
Put extra floor space to use in a larger bathroom with a corner sauna. A unit such as this is an incredible luxury in a bathroom, and even though it can fit up to four people, the corner orientation ensures that the sauna takes up as little floor space as possible. Placing it next to a tub or shower only makes sense because the two experiences go hand in hand.

**TINY SAUNAS WORK IN SMALLER ROOMS.** Incorporate affordable luxury into a large bathroom with a one- or two-person sauna. Smaller and more compact than most units, these can usually fit in a corner or next to a shower enclosure. Many prefab saunas are entirely self-contained—all they need is an electrical outlet. As this one clearly shows, prefabricated units don't sacrifice style to function—they look as nice as they work.

**CONVERT A CLOSET TO A SAUNA.** You may think you don't have the room for a fabulous sauna, but sometimes it's just a matter of looking in the right place. An unused closet next to this bathroom has been converted to a small but serviceable sauna. An integral vent fan and modest heating stove serve the small space well, adding a big touch of luxury to a small room.

▲ **EXPLOIT SHOWER CORNERS.** Corners in shower enclosures are usually just dead space, but not so when you include a handy soap dispenser such as this one. With sections for shampoo, conditioner, and body wash, this dispenser can replace all those bottles that normally clutter up a shelf, alcove, or ledge in the shower. The see-through tubes allow you to monitor the level of your hair- and body-care products, and the chrome body is just bright and shiny enough to add a little sparkle to the enclosure.

▶ **SHELF IT FOR MAJOR CONVENIENCE.** The key challenge in most shower enclosures is finding a place to put all the personal care products you need when showering. Look no further. A shelf like this is meant for use in the shower, with an eminently cleanable plastic-and-stainless-steel construction, and an easy, no-drill adhesive attachment to the wall. The shelf is the perfect size to hold the various items you'll need in the shower, without intruding into the usable showering space.

◄ **PUT SOAPS AND BODY-CARE PRODUCTS RIGHT WHERE YOU NEED THEM.** Dispensers such as these are so handy that you'll wonder how you ever got along without them once they're installed. They stick to the wall without a need for screws or drilling. Each container is easily refilled and a breeze to keep clean—just swipe them off with a washcloth and they look brand new. Handy bottom hooks allow you to hang everything from a washcloth to a razor, to keep essentials right at hand.

▼ **MAKE SHAVING A BREEZE WITH A SPECIAL SHAVING MIRROR.** This acrylic, frameless mirror is an absolute time saver that allows men to shave in the shower. There's no better place for shaving because the beard is already softened. This handy mirror is anti-fogging and lightweight, with its own chrome razor hook. You won't need tools or expertise to install it, and you won't have to permanently alter your tiled wall—its stuck to the wall with two-sided tape and a little silicone seal.

**ADD LIGHT AND AIR FROM ABOVE.** Add a roof window over a shower that needs both light and venting. A roof window is an operable skylight that provides a chance to air out a steamy room while allowing for tons of daylight. Roof windows like this are not terribly hard to install as long as the bathroom is located right underneath the roof rather than under another room.

**INTRODUCE UNEXPECTED ILLUMINATION WITH TUNNEL SKYLIGHTS.** Use tube skylights to light a bathroom with specific spots of daylight. These unique fixtures are literally tunnels routed from a lens in the roof, down through a reflective tube, to a lens in the ceiling. Because of the way the ceiling lens is made and installed, it disperses light and brightens the room far more than the small size would indicate.

**SPREAD THE LIGHT WITH A FLARED SKYLIGHT SHAFT.** Where your bathroom is limited to modest clerestory windows, you can find much-needed natural light by adding a large skylight. The skylight in this room is not only sizable, but it has also been installed in a flared shaft, ensuring the light penetrates throughout the bathroom. Retrofitting your bathroom with a big skylight and flared shaft involves a lot of expense and work, but the stunning benefits are pretty obvious—and obviously pretty.

**TUNNEL SKYLIGHT BEFORE-AND-AFTER.** Brighten any bathroom far beyond what you might anticipate with the addition of tunnel skylights. See the difference between a room lit by artificial fixtures (left) and the same room equipped with a tunnel skylight (right). The difference is astounding.

▲ **MULTIPLY THE LIGHT AND DRAMA WITH UNUSUAL BATHROOM WINDOWS.**
Add windows such as these to not only take advantage of a great view,
but to also frame a stunning tub. Divided panes such as the ones in these
windows add immensely to the bathroom's design, but the real draws
are the view and the light. This type of treatment works best when an
appealing year-round view is available, unencumbered by structures that
might house people looking in.

▶ ▲ **USE GLASS BLOCK TO OPTIMIZE PRIVACY AND LIGHT.** Although glass
block is not as popular as it once was, it remains an excellent material for
a bathroom window. Light, inexpensive, and easy to work with, glass block
achieves the two aims of any bathroom window: it lets the maximum
amount of light into the room, while maintaining the maximum amount
of privacy. Glass block comes in many different surface textures, including
abstract designs and more regular machined textures. You can even
choose colored glass block.

▶ **LET WINDOW WALLS DRIVE THE DESIGN.** Where an opulent spa-like tub
setting abuts a wall, a full-wall window can complete the scene. This is
especially true when the room has a soaring cathedral ceiling. This wall of
glass opens the room and offers a stunning panorama night or day. Half-
height window shades provide privacy as needed and are an excellent
window treatment for any bathroom.

**SOAK A BATHTUB WITH NATURAL LIGHT FROM ABOVE.** Make an attic or top-floor bathroom a stunning sun-washed space by adding basic skylights. The impact of even simple flat skylights is incredibly powerful. At night, these units read black, and artificial light creates a different atmosphere in the room. During the day, the room needs no help to be perfectly illuminated.

**▲ HARDWIRE A TOWEL WARMER FOR AN AFFORDABLE INDULGENCE.** Bring a big touch of luxury to your modest guest bath with a wall-mounted, hardwired towel warmer. A rack such as this can hold many different towels for drying or warming fresh towels, and the chrome finish fits with most bathroom design styles. You can also find white or black versions if that's a better look for your bathroom; choose a plug-in version where you'd prefer not to wire in the unit.

**▶ PICK A TOWEL WARMER TO FIT AVAILABLE SPACE.** When you don't have the room or inclination to add a wall-mounted or freestanding towel warmer rack, it doesn't mean the luxury is lost; a towel-warmer drawer can be easily built into a column of shelves or a linen closet and will keep your towels toasty for extravagant bathing.

▶ **LARGE TOWEL WARMERS SERVE BUSY ROOMS.** Install a full-length towel warmer for all the towel storage you need—including space for both fresh and wet towels. A towel warmer such as the one in this pristine white bathroom can dry and warm towels quickly, and it also adds an interesting ladder-like visual. Wired-in warmers take a little more effort and expense, but the convenience of a warm towel at the flip of a switch is usually well worth the investment.

▼ **USE TOWEL WARMERS AS BACKGROUND ACCENTS.** Choose a towel warmer rack that suits the available space, as well as the style of your bathroom. Here, leopard-print vessel sinks grab most of the attention, and the towel warmer is merely meant to fit in—a role for which the highly adaptable chrome finish is perfectly suited. But the space in this bathroom was constricted, leaving no wall area large enough for a standard-size towel warmer. This narrower version does the job just as well, though, and fits perfectly in a postage-stamp-sized location on the wall.

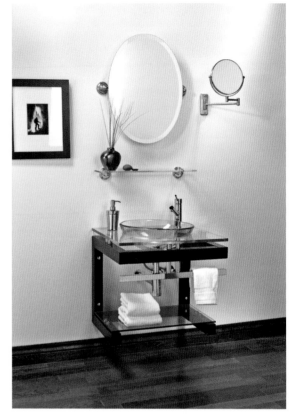

▲ **TILE A MIRROR INTO A WALL.** Blend your mirror into the surroundings—if not the architecture itself—by tiling it into the wall. The myriad tiles on the wall of this bathroom have been laid around the mirror; the edge tiles form a frame around the mirror itself. It's a seamless design choice, and the mirror seems contiguous with the tiled surface.

▶▲ **ADD FUNCTION, FORM, AND VERSATILITY IN ONE WITH A TILTING MIRROR.** If you decide to use a mirror without a medicine chest, your options open up. This oval mirror is attached to pivot mounts, which allow it to be tilted to suit the height of the user. A smaller, wall-mounted personal mirror serves personal grooming chores such as shaving or applying lipstick. The combination of mirrors ensures that this sink is as useful as it is attractive.

▶ **INJECT A BIT OF WHIMSY INTO THE BATHROOM WITH A ROUND MIRROR.** The shape is informal and captures a sense of fun. As this bathroom shows, a round mirror is perfect for a funky design style, which in this case includes unusual pendant lights on each side of the mirror, a metal vessel sink, and a mod wall-mount faucet. The frosted-glass mirror frame complements the other eclectic elements.

**MATCH MIRROR FRAMES TO DISTINCTIVE SURFACES.** Use a mirror frame as the opportunity to accent the room's design and reinforce the style set by the sink and vanity. Here, a rustic wood vanity with copper undermount sink creates a definitive look. The hammered copper mirror frame perfectly complements the look and adds interest around the mirror.

▶ **ADD SOME HANDY TOWEL STORAGE ALONG WITH A SPLASH OF STYLE.** That sad truth in just about every bathroom is that there are not enough places to put dry and wet towels. But this compact, vertical towel rack solves that problem and then some. It provides enough hanging space for a good collection of towels, and the simple chrome construction makes it easy to clean and easy to look at. It's ideal for a smaller bathroom with limited wall space for screw-in towel racks.

▽ **SAVE YOUR WALLS AND ADD FLEXIBILITY AND STORAGE BY USING A TOILET PAPER ROLL TOWER.** This tower, and variations like it, hold toilet paper at the ready and store additional roles in a tiny footprint. Going vertical, the accent is a space saver and fits right in next to a toilet. But it's also an easy alternative to screwing a toilet paper holder to a wall or the side of a vanity. Of course, you may choose to use this more for the form than the function; the simple chrome structure is elegant and appealing to the eye, with a tiny top shelf.

**CONSIDER HOOKS AS DECORATIVE FEATURES.** Add storage and flair to the bathroom with hooks mounted on the walls. Although they are small design additions, they come in a vast variety of styles, finishes, and looks. They are also incredibly handy because hooks can be placed just about anywhere they are needed (including on tiled surfaces). You can add the exact number that suits your purposes; plus they're adaptable—a sturdy, stylish hook such as this can be used to hang towels, a bathrobe, or a suit in preparation for dressing. Hanging it with a witty reference to pegboard surfaces behind it is a wonderful added touch.

**EVEN HANDLES AND KNOBS PRESENT DESIGN OPPORTUNITIES.** Accessorize your bathroom with door and drawer handles that say "special" in subtle ways. You would expect to find crystal handles like these on a dresser or nightstand. Added to vanity doors, the handles delight the eye and add points of sparkle in the bathroom—an outsized effect for such a small decorative feature. Handles are the perfect decorative feature with which to experiment in the bathroom because they are inexpensive and so easy to change.

**MATCH ACCENT FINISHES TO FAUCETS AND FIXTURES.** Antique finishes have become more and more popular for the bathroom, not only for faucets but also for matching accents as well. This towel and hook combo shows the fine detailing available in accents, with slight distressing of the finish that makes the pieces look authentically antique. You'll find these types of accents available in copper tones, nickel, and stainless steel surfaces, and even brass and gold.

**ACCESSORIZE DRAWER PULLS, KNOBS, OR OTHER BATHROOM HANDLES OR SPOUTS.** Special drawer pulls are your way of adding a bit of flash to an otherwise visually sedate or subtle cabinet or vanity. Special design features, such as the tiny row of crystals in the center of these pulls, are ideal because the audience in a bathroom is often captive due to the functions of the room. Unexpected design flashes are a real treat to the eye and have outsized visual power in the limited space of a bathroom.

# RESOURCES

**American Institute of Architects (AIA)**
Their website includes information on Universal Design principles and resources and a list of members who practice Universal Design architecture.
www.aia.org
(202) 626-7300

**American Association of Retired Persons (AARP)**
Provides articles and information on Universal Design to accommodate elderly and disabled living.
www.aarp.org
(888) OUR-AARP

**American Society of Interior Designers (ASID)**
The society provides consumers with information about bathroom design, Universal Design practice, and implementation in the design, and a list of designers.
www.asid.org
(202) 546-3480

**The Energy & Environmental Building Alliance (EEBA)**
This organization offers networking and educational resources in promotion of sustainable building practices.
www.eeba.org
(952) 881-1098

**National Association of the Remodeling Industry (NARI)**
Offers comprehensive information on budgeting, planning, and executing home remodeling projects, including bathroom redesigns, additions and remodels. The website provides listings of membercontractors of all types.
www.nari.org
(847) 298-9200

**National Kitchen & Bath Association (NKBA)**
The NKBA inspires homeowners with a gallery of stunning bathroom designs, helps you plan and design your own bathroom remodel and provides contact information for professionals that can help you bring it all together.
www.nkba.org
(800) 843-6522

**United States Environmental Protection Agency—Indoor Air Quality**
In-depth information about materials and practices—including bathroom design concerns such as mold—that affect indoor air quality in homes nationwide.
www.epa.gov

**United States Green Building Council**
A nonprofit dedicated to educating and helping consumers remodel, design, build, and live in more environmentally friendly homes.
www.usgbc.org
(800) 795-1747

# PHOTO CREDITS

Page 4 bottom: Photo courtesy of Brizo®, brizo.com, (877) 345-2749

Page 5 top: Photo courtesy of Pfister, www.pfisterfaucets.com, (800) 732-8238

Page 6 top: Photo courtesy of Durat, www.durat.com and Modern Surfaces, www.modern-surfaces.com

Page 6 bottom: Photo courtesy of Merillat® Cabinetry, www.merillat.com

Page 7 top: Photo courtesy of Delta Faucet, www.deltafaucet.com, (800) 345-3358

Page 7 bottom: Photo courtesy of Crossville, Inc., www.crossvilleinc.com, (931) 484-2110

Page 8 top: Photo by Alexey Kuznetso, www.istock.com

Page 8 bottom right: Photo courtesy of Fairmont Designs, www.fairmontdesigns.com, (714) 670-1171

Page 8 bottom left: Photo courtesy of Encore Cabinetry, www.encoreceramics.com

Page 9: Photo courtesy of American Standard Brands, www.americanstandard-us.com, (800) 442-1902

Page 10 top: Photo courtesy of Pfister, www.pfisterfaucets.com, (800) 732-8238

Page 10 bottom: Photo courtesy of Bestbath, bestbath.com, (800) 727-9907

Page 11 top: Photo courtesy of American Standard Brands, www.americanstandard-us.com, (800) 442-1902

Page 12: Photo courtesy of Fairmount Designs, www.fairmountdesigns.com (714) 670-1171

Page 13 top: Photo courtesy of American Standard Brands, www.americanstandard-us.com, (800) 442-1902

Page 13: Photo courtesy of Krull & Associates for Geberit; courtesy of Lacava, www.lacava.com

Page 14 top: Photo courtesy of GROHE www.grohe.com/us

Page 14 bottom: Photo courtesy of Brizo®, brizo.com, (877) 345-2749

Page 15: Photo courtesy of Benjamin Moore, www.benjaminmoore.com, (855) 724-6802

Page 16: Photo by John Wollwerth/ www.shutterstock.com

Page 17 top right: Photo by Pics721/ www.shutterstock.com

Page 17 top left: Photo by Vince Clements / www.shutterstock.com

Page 17 bottom left: Photo by Linerpics / www.shutterstock.com

Page 18: Photo courtesy of Pfister, www.pfisterfaucets.com, (800) 732-8238

Page 18 bottom: Photo courtesy of Rev-A-Shelf, www.rev-a-shelf.com, (800) 626-1126

Page 19: Photo courtesy of Lacava, www.lacava.com, (888) 522-2823

Page 20 top: Photo courtesy of American Standard, www.americanstandard.com, (800) 442-1902

Page 21 top: Photo courtesy of Creative Publishing International

Page 21 bottom: Photo courtesy of Pyrolave, www.pyrolaveUSA.com

Page 22: Photo courtesy by Andrea Rugg for Otogawa-Anschel Design and Build

Page 23: Photo courtesy of Kohler, www.kohlerco.com, (800) 4KOHLER

Page 24 top left: Photo courtesy of Bestbath, bestbath.com, (800) 727-9907

Page 24 top right: Photo by Iriana Shiya / www.Shutterstock.com

Page 24 bottom: Photo courtesy of Kohler, www.kohlerco.com, (800) 4KOHLER

Page 25 top: Photo courtesy of Merillat® Cabinetry, www.merillat.com

Page 25 bottom: Photo courtesy of American Standard Brands, www.americanstandard-us.com, (800) 442-1902

Page 26 top: Photo courtesy of Merillat® Cabinetry, www.merillat.com

Page 26 bottom: Photo courtesy of Coastal Shower Doors, coastalshowerdoors.com, (800) 874-8601

Page 27: Photo courtesy of Quality Cabinet, www.qualitycabinets.com

Page 28: Photo courtesy of Caesarstone, www.caesarstoneus.com

Page 29 top: Photo courtesy of Merillat® Cabinetry, www.merillat.com

Page 29 bottom: Photo courtesy of American Standard Brands, www.americanstandard-us.com, (800) 442-1902

Page 30 top: Photo courtesy of Merillat® Cabinetry, www.merillat.com

Page 30 bottom: Photo courtesy of Crossville, Inc., www.crossvilleinc.com, (931) 484-2110

Page 31 top: Photo courtesy of Hansgrohe, www.hansgrohe-usa.com, (800) 334-0455

Page 31 bottom: Photo courtesy of Grohe, www.groheamerica.com, (630) 582-7711

Page 32: Photo courtesy of Brizo®, brizo.com, (877) 345-2749

Page 33: Photo courtesy of Caesarstone, www.caesarstoneus.com

Page 34 top: Photo courtesy of Icera, www.icerausa.com, (855) 444-2372

Page 34 bottom: Photo courtesy of BainUltra, www.bainultra.com, (800) 463-2187

Page 35: Photo courtesy of Lacava, www.lacava.com, (888) 522-2823

Page 36: Photo courtesy of Bestbath, bestbath.com, (800) 727-9907

Page 37: Photo courtesy of Kohler, www.kohlerco.com, (800) 4 KOHLER

Page 38 top right: Photo by Eric Roth

Page 38 bottom: Photo courtesy of Ceramic Tiles of Italy, www.italiatiles.com

Page 39: Photo courtesy of Ceramic Tiles of Italy, www.italiatiles.com

Page 40: Photo courtesy of Caesarstone, www.caesarstoneus.com

Page 41 top: Photo courtesy of Pfister, www.pfisterfaucets.com, (800) 732-8238

Page 41 bottom left: Photo courtesy of Lacava, www.lacava.com, (888) 522-2823

Page 41 bottom right: Photo courtesy of BainUltra, www.bainultra.com, (800) 463-2187

Page 42: Photo courtesy of Infinity Drain, infinitydrain.com, (516) 767-6786

Page 43: Photo courtesy of Ceramic Tiles of Italy, www.italiatiles.com

Page 45 top left and right: Photo courtesy of Ceramic Tiles of Italy, www.italiatiles.com

Page 45 bottom left: Creative Publishing international

Page 45 bottom right: Creative Publishing international

Pages 46-47, all: Creative Publishing international

Page 48 top: Photo courtesy of Bestbath, bestbath.com, (800) 727-9907

Page 48 bottom: Photo courtesy of BR-111, www.br111.com, (800) 525-2711

Page 49: Photo courtesy of Crossville, Inc., www.crossvilleinc.com, (931) 484-2110

Page 50 top: Photo courtesy of American Standard Brands, www.americanstandard-us.com, (800) 442-1902

Page 50 bottom left: Photo courtesy of Oceanside Glasstile™, www.glasstile.com, (760) 929-5882

Page 50 bottom right: Photo courtesy of Ikea Home Furnishings, www.ikea-USA.com, (610) 834-0180

Page 51 top: Photo courtesy of Hakatai Enterprises, www.hakatai.com, (888) 667-2429

Page 51 bottom left: Felix-Andrei Constantinescu / www.Shutterstock.com

Page 51 bottom right: Photo courtesy of Hakatai Enterprises, www.hakatai.com, (888) 667-2429

Page 52 top right: Photo courtesy of Victoria + Albert, www.vandabaths.com

Page 52 top right: Photo courtesy of Jacuzzi, www.jacuzzi.com, (909) 606-1416

Page 52 bottom: Photo by Linerpics / www.shutterstock.com

Page 53 bottom: Photo courtesy of Lacava, www.lacava.com, (888) 522-2823

Page 54: Photo by Baloncici / www.Shutterstock.com

Page 55 left: Photo courtesy of Merillat® Cabinetry, www.merillat.com

Page 55 right: Photo courtesy of Hakatai Enterprises, www.hakatai.com, (888) 667-2429

Page 56 top: Photo courtesy of Native Trails, Inc., www.nativetrails.net, (800) 786-0862

Page 56 bottom: Photo courtesy of Pyrolave USA, www.pyrolave.com

Page 57: Photo courtesy of ThinkGlass, www.thinkglass.com, (877) 410-4527

Page 58 top: Photo courtesy of Stuart Watson, designed by David Reaume, www.walkerzanger.com

Page 58 bottom: Photo courtesy of Caesarstone, www.caesarstoneus.com

Page 59: Photo courtesy of Isenberg, www.isenbergfaucets.com, (972) 510-5916

Page 60: Photo by Magdalena Bujak / www.Shutterstock.com

Page 61: Photo courtesy of Kallista, www.kallista.com, (888) 452-5547

Page 62: Photo courtesy of Lacava, www.lacava.com, (888) 522-2823

Page 63: Photo courtesy of American Standard Brands, www.americanstandard-us.com, (800) 442-1902

Page 64 top left: Photo courtesy of Diamond Cabinets, www.diamond2.com

Page 64 top right: Photo courtesy of Madelli, Inc., www.madeli.com, (800) 819-6988

Page 64 bottom: Photo courtesy of Fairmont Designs, www.fairmontdesigns.com, (714) 670-1171

Page 65 top: Photo courtesy of Diamond Cabinets,m www.diamond2.com

Page 65 bottom left: Photo courtesy of Native Trails, Inc., www.nativetrails.net, (800) 786-0862

Page 65 bottom right: Photo courtesy of Native Trails, Inc., www.nativetrails.net, (800) 786-0862

Page 66: Photo by Francesco Grossi; design by Paolo Demarco, courtesy of Lacava, www.lacava.com, (888) 522-2823

Page 67 top right: Photo courtesy of Fairmont Designs, www.fairmontdesigns.com, (714) 670-1171

Page 67 top left: Photo courtesy of Madelli, Inc., www.madeli.com, (800) 819-6988

Page 67 bottom: Photo courtesy of Madelli, Inc., www.madeli.com, (800) 819-6988

Page 68 top left: Photo courtesy of Xylem Group, LLC, www.xylem.biz, (866) 395-8112

Page 68 top right: Photo courtesy of Xylem Group, LLC, www.xylem.biz, (866) 395-8112

Page 68 bottom: Photo courtesy of Brizo®, brizo.com, (877) 345-2749

Page 69: Photo courtesy of Fairmont Designs, www.fairmontdesigns.com, (714) 670-1171

Page 70: Photo courtesy of Rev-A-Shelf, www.rev-a-shelf.com, (800) 626-1126

Page 71: Photo courtesy of The Furniture Guild, www.thefurnitureguild.com, (888) 479-4108

Page 72 top: Photo courtesy of Merillat® Cabinetry, www.merillat.com

Page 72 bottom left: Photo courtesy of Madelli, Inc., www.madeli.com, (800) 819-6988

Page 72 bottom right: Photo courtesy of Fairmont Designs, www.fairmontdesigns.com, (714) 670-1171

Page73 top left: Photo courtesy of Madelli, Inc., www.madeli.com, (800) 819-6988

Page 73 top right: Photo courtesy of Madelli, Inc., www.madeli.com, (800) 819-6988

Page 73 bottom: Photo courtesy of Caesarstone, www.caesarstoneus.com

Page 74: Photo courtesy of Lacava, www.lacava.com, (888) 522-2823

Page 75: Photo courtesy of Merillat® Cabinetry, www.merillat.com

Page 76: Photo courtesy of Merillat® Cabinetry, www.merillat.com

Page 77 top: Photo courtesy of Moen, www.moen.com, (800) 289-6636

Page77 bottom: Photo courtesy of Hansgrohe, www.hansgrohe-usa.com, (800) 334-0455

Page 78 top left: Photo courtesy of American Standard, www.americanstandard.com, (800) 442-1902

Page 79: Photo courtesy of BainUltra, Inc., www.bainultra.com, (800) 463-2187

Page 80 top: Photo courtesy of Sunrise Specialty Company, www.sunrisespecialty.com, (800) 444-4280

Page 80 bottom: Photo courtesy of Native Trails, Inc., www.nativetrails.net, (800) 786-0862

Page 81 top: Photo courtesy of Kohler, www.kohlerco.com, (800) 4 KOHLER

Page 81 bottom: Photo by Andrea Rugg for David Hiede Design

Page 82 top: Photo courtesy of Victoria + Albert, www.vandabaths.com

Page 82 bottom left: Photo courtesy of Victoria + Albert, www.vandabaths.com

Page 82 bottom right: Photo by LuckyPhoto/ www.Shutterstock.com

Page 83: Photo by Marcos Sabugo, Photographer, www.marcossabugo.com, (561) 352-5585

Page 84: Photo courtesy of Native Trails, Inc., www.nativetrails.net, (800) 786-0862

Page 85: Photo courtesy of BainUltra, www.bainultra.com, (800) 463-2187

Page 86 -87, all: Photo courtesy of Eago USA, eagousa.com, (800) 990-ALFI

Page 88 top: Photo courtesy of American Standard Brands, www.americanstandard-us.com, (800) 463-2187

Page 88 bottom: Photo courtesy of Kohler, www.kohlerco.com, (800) 4 KOHLER

Page 89: Photo courtesy of BainUltra, www.bainultra.com, (800) 463-2187

Page 90 top: Photo by Karen Melvin

Page 90 bottom: Photo courtesy of Eago USA, eagousa.com, (800) 990-ALFI

Page 91 top: Photo courtesy of BainUltra, www.bainultra.com, (800) 463-2187

Page 91 bottom: Photo courtesy of Caesarstone, www.caesarstoneus.com

Page 92: Photo courtesy of Jacuzzi, www.jacuzzi.com, (909) 606-1416

Page 93 top: Photo courtesy of Diamond Spas, www.diamondspas.com

Page 93 bottom: Photo courtesy of MTI Whirlpools

Page 94 top: Photo courtesy of BainUltra, www.bainultra.com, (800) 463-2187

Page 94 bottom: Photo courtesy of American Standard, www.americanstandard.com, (800) 442-1902

Page 95: Photo courtesy of BainUltra, www.bainultra.com, (800) 463-2187

Page 96 top: Photo courtesy of American Standard Brands, www.americanstandard-us.com, (800) 442-1902

Page 96 bottom: Photo courtesy of Infinity Drain, infinitydrain.com, (516) 767-6786

Page 97: Photo courtesy of Kallista, www.kallista.com, (888) 452-5547

Page 98 left: Photo courtesy of BathAid, bathaid.com, (844) 228-4243

Page 98 right: Photo courtesy of Bestbath, bestbath.com, (800) 727-9907

Page 99 top: Photo courtesy of Jacuzzi, www.jacuzzi.com, (909) 606-1416

Page 99 bottom: Photo courtesy of Bestbath, bestbath.com, (800) 727-9907

Page 100: Photo courtesy of Crossville, Inc., www.crossvilleinc.com, (931) 484-2110

Page 101 top: Photo courtesy of Hansgrohe, www.hansgrohe-usa.com, (800) 334-0455

Page 101 bottom: Photo courtesy of QuickDrain USA, www.quickdrainusa.com, (866) 998-6685

Page 102: Photo courtesy of American Standard Brands, www.americanstandard-us.com, (800) 442-1902

Page 103 top: Photo courtesy of Bestbath, bestbath.com, (800) 727-9907

Page 103 bottom: Photo courtesy of Caesarstone, www.caesarstoneus.com

Page 104 left: Photo courtesy of Hakatai Enterprises, www.hakatai.com, (888) 667-2429

Page 104 right: Photo courtesy of Hakatai Enterprises, www.hakatai.com, (888) 667-2429

Page 105, all: Photo courtesy of Infinity Drain, infinitydrain.com, (516) 767-6786

Page 106: Photo courtesy of Hakatai Enterprises, www.hakatai.com, (888) 667-2429

Page 107 top: Photo courtesy of American Standard, www.americanstandard.com, (800) 442-1902

Page 107 bottom left: Photo courtesy of Bestbath, bestbath.com, (800) 727-9907

Page 107 bottom right: Photo courtesy of Bestbath, bestbath.com, (800) 727-9907

Page 108, all: Photo courtesy of Bestbath, bestbath.com, (800) 727-9907

Page 110: Photo courtesy of Sunrise Specialty Company, www.sunrisespecialty.com, (800) 444-4280

Page 111: Photo courtesy of GROHE www.grohe.com/us/

Page 112 left: Photo courtesy of Infinity Drain, infinitydrain.com, (516) 767-6786

Page 112 right: Photo courtesy of Kallista, www.kallista.com, (888) 452-5547

Page 113 top: Photo courtesy of Better Living Products, www.betterlivingproducts.ca, (800) 487-3300

Page 113 bottom: Photo courtesy of Kallista, www.kallista.com, (888) 452-5547

Page 114: Photo courtesy of American Standard, www.americanstandard.com, (800) 442-1902

Page 115: Photo courtesy of Lacava, www.lacava.com, (888) 522-2823

Page 116: Photo courtesy of American Standard Brands, www.americanstandard-us.com, (800) 442-1902

Page 117 left: Photo by Nomad_Soul / www.Shutterstock.com

Page 117 middle: www.Shutterstock.com

Page 117 right: Photo by Photobank.ch / www.Shutterstock.com

Page 118: Photo courtesy of Lacava, www.lacava.com, (888) 522-2823

Page 119 top: Photo courtesy of Icera, www.icerausa.com, (855) 444-2372

Page 119 bottom: Photo courtesy of Kallista.com, (888) 452-5547

Page 120, all: Photo courtesy of Madelli, Inc., www.madeli.com, (800) 819-6988

Page 121: Photo courtesy of Native Trails, Inc., www.nativetrails.net, (800) 786-0862

Page 121 bottom: Photo by Trubach / www.Shutterstock.com

Page 122- 124, all: Photo courtesy of Native Trails, Inc., www.nativetrails.net, (800) 786-0862

Page 125 top: Photo courtesy of Lacava, www.lacava.com, (888) 522-2823

Page 125 bottom: Photo courtesy of Native Trails, Inc., www.nativetrails.net, (800) 786-0862

Page 126: Photo courtesy of Brizo®, brizo.com, (877) 345-2749

Page 127 top: Photo courtesy of Grohe, www.groheamerica.com, (630) 582-7711

Page 127 bottom left: Photo courtesy of Native Trails, Inc., www.nativetrails.net, (800) 786-0862

Page 127 bottom right: Photo courtesy of Lacava, www.lacava.com, (888) 522-2823

Page 128: Photo courtesy of GROHE www.grohe.com/us/

Page 129 top: Photo by Rodho / www.Shutterstock.com

Page 129 bottom: Photo by Yampi / www.Shutterstock.com

Page 130 top: Photo courtesy of Jacuzzi, www.jacuzzi.com, (909) 606-1416

Page 130 bottom: Photo courtesy of American Standard Brands, www.americanstandard-us.com, (800) 442-1902

Page 131: Photo courtesy of Native Trails, Inc., www.nativetrails.net, (800) 786-0862

Page 132: Photo by Francesco Grossi; design by Paolo Demarco, courtesy of Lacava, www.lacava.com, (888) 522-2823

Page 133 top left: Photo by Jocic / www.Shutterstock.com

Page 133 top right: Photo by Yuyangc / www.Shutterstock.com

Page 133 bottom: Photo by Terekhov Igor / www.Shutterstock.com

Page 134 top: Photo courtesy of Lenova, www.lenovasinks.com, (877) 733-1098

Page 134 bottom: Photo courtesy of Native Trails, Inc., www.nativetrails.net, (800) 786-0862

Page 135 top: Photo courtesy of Ceramic Tiles of Italy, www.italiatiles.com

Page 135 bottom: Photo courtesy of Native Trails, Inc., www.nativetrails.net, (800) 786-0862

Page 136 bottom left: Photo courtesy of Madelli, Inc., www.madeli.com, (800) 819-6988

Page 136 bottom right: Photo courtesy of Pyrolave USA, www.pyrolave.com

Page 137: Photo courtesy of Native Trails, Inc., www.nativetrails.net, (800) 786-0862

Page 138 top left: Photo by Baloncici / www.Shutterstock.com

Page 138 top right: Photo courtesy of Champlain Stone, Ltd., www.champlainstone.com, (518) 623-2902

Page 138 bottom: Photo courtesy of Kohler, www.kohlerco.com, (800) 4 KOHLER

Page 139 top: Photo courtesy of Xylem Group, LLC, www.xylem.biz, (866) 395-8112

Page 139 bottom left: Creative Publishing international

Page 139 bottom right: Photo courtesy of Kohler, www.kohlerco.com, (800) 4 KOHLER Page 130: Rehan Qureshi / www.Shutterstock.com

Page 140: Photo courtesy of Isenberg, www.isenbergfaucets.com, (972) 510-5916

Page 140: Photo by Linerpics / www.Shutterstock.com

Page 141: Photo courtesy of Pyrolave, www.pyrolaveUSA.com

Page 142: Photo courtesy of Brizo®, brizo.com, (877) 345-2749

Page 143: Photo courtesy of Hansgrohe, www.hansgrohe-usa.com, (800) 334-0455

Page 144 top left: Photo courtesy of Moen, www.moen.com, (800) 289-6636

Page 144 top right: Photo courtesy of Kohler, www.kohlerco.com, (800) 4 KOHLER

Page 144 bottom: Photo courtesy of Grohe, www.groheamerica.com, (630) 582-7711

Page 145 top: Photo courtesy of Native Trails, Inc., www.nativetrails.net, (800) 786-0862

Page 145 bottom left: Photo courtesy of Kohler, www.kohlerco.com, (800) 4 KOHLER

Page 145 bottom right: Photo courtesy of Hansgrohe, www.hansgrohe-usa.com, (800) 334-0455

Page 146 top: Photo courtesy of Grohe, www.groheamerica.com, (630) 582-7711

Page 146 bottom left: Photo courtesy of Pfister, www.pfisterfaucets.com, (800) 732-8238

Page 146 bottom right: Photo courtesy of Pfister, www.pfisterfaucets.com, (800) 732-8238

Page 147: Photo courtesy of Native Trails, Inc., www.nativetrails.net, (800) 786-0862

Page 148: Photo courtesy of Durat, www.durat.com and Modern Surfaces, www.modern-surfaces.com

Page 149 top: Photo courtesy of Delta Faucet, www.deltafaucet.com, (800) 345-3358

Page 149 bottom: Photo courtesy of Pfister, www.pfisterfaucets.com, (800) 732-8238

Page 150 top: Photo courtesy of Pfister, www.pfisterfaucets.com, (800) 732-8238

Page 150 bottom: Photo courtesy of Brizo®, brizo.com, (877) 345-2749

Page 151: Creative Publishing International

Page 152- 153, all: Photo courtesy of Kallista, www.kallista.com, (888) 452-5547

Page 154: Photo courtesy of American Standard Brands, www.americanstandard-us.com, (800) 442 1902

Page 155 top left: Photo courtesy of Kohler, www.kohlerco.com, (800) 4 KOHLER

Page 155 top right: Photo courtesy of Delta Faucet, www.deltafaucet.com, (800) 345-3358

Page 155 bottom right: Photo courtesy of Grohe, www.groheamerica.com, (630) 582-7711

Page 156 left: Photo courtesy of Hakatai Enterprises, www.hakatai.com,(888) 667-2429

Page 156 bottom right: Photo courtesy of Brizo, www.brizo.com

Page 157 top: Creative Publishing international

Page 157 bottom: Photo courtesy of Alfi Trade, Inc., alfitrade.com

Page 158 top left: Photo courtesy of Grohe, www.groheamerica.com, (630) 582-7711

Page 158 top right: Photo courtesy of Native Trails, Inc., www.nativetrails.net, (800) 786-0862

Page 158 bottom: Photo courtesy of Bestbath, bestbath.com, (800) 727-9907

Page 159 top: Photo courtesy of Ceramic Tiles of Italy, www.italiatiles.com

Page 159 bottom left: Photo courtesy of Jacuzzi, www.jacuzzi.com, (909) 606-1416

Page 159 right: Photo courtesy of Kohler, www.kohlerco.com, (800) 4 KOHLER

Page 160: Photo by Jessie Walker

Page 161 top: Photo by Ioana Davies (Drutu) / www.Shutterstock.com

Page 161 bottom left: Photo courtesy of Crossville, Inc., www.crossvilleinc.com, (931) 484-2110

Page 161 bottom right: Photo by Ventura / www.Shutterstock.com

Page 162 top left: Photo courtesy of Broan-NuTone, www.broan.com, (800) 558-1711

Page 162 top right: Photo courtesy of Broan-NuTone, www.broan.com, (800) 558-1711

Page 162 bottom: Creative Publishing international

Page 163 top: Photo by Tr1sha / www.Shutterstock.com

Page 163 bottom: Photo by Roseburn3DStudio / www.Shutterstock.com

Page 164: Photo courtesy of Hakatai Enterprises, www.hakatai.com, (888) 667-2429

Page 165: Photo courtesy of Crossville, Inc., www.crossvilleinc.com, (931) 484-2110

Page 167 top: Photo courtesy of BathAid, bathaid.com, (844) 228-4243

Page 167 bottom: Photo courtesy of Moen, www.moen.com, (800) 289-6636

Page 168 right: Photo courtesy of Harrell Remodeling, Inc/ www.harrell-remodeling.com

Page 168 left: Photo courtesy of Moen, www.moen.com, (800) 289-6636

Page 169: Photo courtesy of Moen, www.moen.com, (800) 289-6636

Page 170 top: Photo courtesy of Bestbath, bestbath.com, (800) 727-9907

Page 170 bottom: Photo courtesy of BathAid, bathaid.com, (844) 228-4243

Page 171-172, all: Photo courtesy of Bestbath, bestbath.com, (800) 727-9907

Page 173: Photo courtesy of Merillat® Cabinetry, www.merillat.com

Page 174 top: Photo by aaphotograph / www.Shutterstock.com

Page 174 bottom: Photo courtesy of Finnleo Sauna and Steam/Saunatec, Inc.

Page 175 top: Photo courtesy of Ideal Standard International/www.idealstandard.com

Page 175 bottom: photosphobos / www.Shutterstock.com

Page 176-177, all: Photo courtesy of Better Living Products, www.betterlivingproducts.ca, (800) 487-3300

Page 178: Photo courtesy of VELUX America Inc., www.veluxusa.com, (800) 888-3589

Page 179 top left: Photo by Istock / www.istock.com

Page 179 top right: Photo courtesy of Solatube International, Inc., www.solatube.com, (888) 765-2882

Page 179 bottom left: Photo courtesy of Solatube International, Inc., www.solatube.com, (888) 765-2882

Page 179 bottom right: Photo courtesy of Solatube International, Inc., www.solatube.com, (888) 765-2882

Page 180 bottom left: Photo courtesy of Pittsburgh Corning Corporation, www.pittsburghcorning.com (800) 732-2499

Page 180 bottom right: Photo by Linda Oyama Bryan

Page 181: Photo courtesy of Hakatai Enterprises, www.hakatai.com, (888) 667-2429

Page 182 top: Creative Publishing international

Page 182 bottom: Photo courtesy of Jacuzzi, www.jacuzzi.com, (909) 606-1416

Page 183 top: Photo by David Hughes / www.Shutterstock.com

Page 183 bottom: Photo by Rade Kovac / www.Shutterstock.com

Page 184 top left: Photo courtesy of Stone & Pewter Accents, www.stonepewteraccents.com, (310) 257-1300

Page 184 top right: Creative Publishing international

Page 184 bottom: Photo by Eric Roth

Page 185: Photo courtesy of Native Trails, Inc., www.nativetrails.net, (800) 786-0862

Page 186 top: Photo courtesy of Lacava, www.lacava.com, (888) 522-2823

Page 186 bottom: Photo courtesy of Better Living Products, www.betterlivingproducts.ca, (800) 487-3300

Page 187: Photo courtesy of Hansgrohe, www.hansgrohe-usa.com, (800) 334-0455

Page 188: Photo courtesy of Atlas Homewares, www.atlashomewares.com, (800) 799-6755

Page 189 top: Photo courtesy of Moen, www.moen.com, (800) 289-6636

Page 189 bottom: Photo courtesy of Atlas Homewares, www.atlashomewares.com, (800) 799-6755